THE MODERN WOMAN'S FRUGAL WEDDING, PALEO DIET NUTRITION, AND MINIMALISM BUNDLE

RACHEL HATHAWAY

RH MEDIA

Published by RH Media. *Version 1.1*

ISBN-13: 978-1547225637
ISBN-10: 1547225637

CONTENTS

Introduction   v
Also by Rachel Hathaway   vii

MINIMALISM FOR MOMS

1. Chapter One: Introduction   5
2. Chapter Two: What Exactly Is Minimalism?   9
3. Chapter Three: All Your Stuff   13
4. Chapter Four: Spending Your Time & Money Wisely   31
   Your Opinion   45
   About the Author   47

UPDATED PALEO DIET FOOD LIST

Feedback   51
Preface   53
Introduction   55
1. Fresh Fruits & Vegetables   59
2. Meats   65
3. Fish & Seafood   69
4. Eggs   73
5. Nuts & Seeds   75
6. Healthy Oils & Fats   77
7. Food to Avoid on a Paleo Diet   79
8. Paleo Diet Food Shopping List Samples   83
9. Closing Thoughts   87
   Did You Like This?   89
   About the Author: Rachel Hathaway   91

Also by Rachel Hathaway   93
Language Preview   95

YOUR $1500 FRUGAL WEDDING

Preface   103
Introduction   105
1. Your Budget   109
2. Venue & Transportation   119
3. Food & Drinks   125
4. Invitations   131
5. The Happy Couple   135
6. Hair and Makeup   143
7. Bridesmaids & Groomsmen   145
8. Centerpieces, Favors, & Decor   147
9. Flowers   153
10. Officiant   157
11. The Photographer   159
12. The Music   163
13. Rehearsal Dinner & Post-Wedding Brunch   167
14. Final Thoughts   171
Frugal Wedding Resources   177
About the Author   179
Also by Rachel Hathaway   181
Notes on My Big Day   183

Afterword   185
Also by Rachel Hathaway   187

INTRODUCTION

I WANT TO THANK YOU and congratulate you for reading this three-book set covering the basics of a wonderful, but frugal wedding, the basics of understanding what you can eat on a Paleo Diet, and an introduction to minimalism for your home life — whether you are a Mom now, or will be at some point in the future.

This book bundle contains proven steps and strategies on how to save money with your wedding (or a friend or relative's wedding!), eat and shop wisely, and regain a sense of balance and serenity in your life and in your home. Here's an inescapable fact: you will need put these ideas into action for them to have a real impact on your life, but if you do, you will see results. That's what I've experienced in my life!

It's time for you to dive right into the three short books contained in this set!

ALSO BY RACHEL HATHAWAY

Updated Paleo Diet Food List (Plus Paleo Diet Shopping Lists)

Beginner's Guide to Writing and Self-Publishing Romance eBooks (New Romance Writer Series) *[Also in paperback]*

Minimalism for Moms: Simplify, Declutter, and Organize Your Way to a Stress Free and Meaningful Life (Serenity at Home)

The Unofficial History of Flirting: Plus Five Ways to Reinvent Valentine's Day and Flirt Like a Bird! (Sassy Girl Series) *[Also in paperback]*

SPANISH TRANSLATIONS (Elisa Prada, translator):

Lista de alimentos para la dieta Paleo: Actualizado / Spanish Language Edition (Updated Paleo Diet Food List Book) (Serie de Nutrición) (Spanish Edition) *[Also in paperback]*

Minimalismo para Mamás: Simplifica, arregla, y organiza tu camino hacia una vida plena libre de estrés (Minimalism for Moms / Spanish edition) (Serie Serenidad en el Hogar)

Minimalism
for Moms

Simplify, Declutter, and
Organize Your Way to
A Stress Free and
Meaningful Life

Rachel Hathaway

Minimalism for Moms: Simplify, Declutter, and Organize Your Way to a Stress-Free and Meaningful Life

Thanks for supporting my work!
Published by RH MEDIA.

This project is for my amazing family, in gratitude for the ever-increasing love and support I receive from them.

CHAPTER ONE: INTRODUCTION

*T*his is what we all want... simplicity! Do you ever stop and realize that what you're doing is *really not working*?

You have too much stuff, too much stress in your life, too much clutter throughout your home, and not enough peace of mind. You need to *stop* the cycle now before your kids end up the same way! Minimalism is the approach you need. You *can* declutter and simplify your life! Learn how to get your kids and your spouse involved in improving your family's quality of life by removing what is unimportant, useless, and unnecessary to your overall happiness. Does your marriage suffer because you are constantly frazzled?

You *need* simplicity... and balance.

This book is a quick introduction to the basic principles of minimalism, with helpful strategies for busy moms on how to thoughtfully and efficiently declutter your house, work, your schedule, your budget, and your life. Read this quick book today and make changes right away!

Hey busy mom! Thanks for getting my new book!

Clutter.

Even the word is closed and unforgiving. Go ahead – say it out loud. There is just *no room* to stretch in that word. No inviting, open space... (sound like your life???)

Room.

Now that word is way better. That "oo" sound is so calming – just like when you first get into a hot bubble bath, or the first few rubs of a great massage... (Yeah right! As if us moms ever have time for that!)

Do you?

- *Ever find yourself screaming (or wanting to scream but you don't dare because you'll wake the baby) "This is not working!"*

- *Hold on to things just because they "might come in handy someday?"*

- *Never get rid of something just because it was a gift and you don't want to hurt that person's feelings?*

- *Keep things that you don't use because "it would be a waste of money to get rid of it?"*

- Wish you could spend more time with just your family, but feel obligated to go to everything you and your spouse and kids get invited to?

- Spend nearly all of your "spare" time organizing and cleaning your house?

If the answer to any of these questions is yes, then you need to declutter and simplify your life!

I already hear the skeptics (yes you!) saying, "This won't help me."

You're right.

This book – by itself – won't help you. You have to help you.

This book is just an introduction to a different way of living and thinking about your life and everything in it. I've included some actions that have helped me and my family achieve a better balance, but this is not a checklist that once you've completed it you automatically become a "Certified Minimalist." Only you are capable of evaluating your life and daily routines and identifying the ways you can live more with less. You are the one who is going to have to decide if this is the right path for you, and actually make the changes.

But don't you think – even for a minute – that you're not capable of this.

You can do it!!

No one is more qualified to make your life better than you are. You are your own expert. You know the best ways to take these ideas and actually translate them into your own life. Believe me when I say that once you've reached the other side of purging, donating, and reprioritizing your life to revolve around less stuff and less activities, you will never regret it! Once you've lived for a few weeks in a spacious and tidy house, and actually spent a few hours with your family without thinking about how you should be dusting, you'll never want to return to those stress-filled days again.

So take a deep breath, remember that nearly everyone goes through this at some point (particularly us moms because we just *love* taking on too much and proving that we're superwomen), grab a cup of tea or coffee (or something stronger if you need it!), push the laundry off the couch, and let's start with the basics...

CHAPTER TWO: WHAT EXACTLY IS MINIMALISM?

*M*inimalism can mean different things to different people, but in essence it is a philosophy of living a simple and well balanced life with *more*.

Wait a minute. What? I thought minimalism was about less?

Believe me: minimalism is about living with **more**...

- More quality time with family and friends
- More space
- More money saved
- More of everything that is truly important to you

So how do you get to this magical place? By embracing the power of **less**...

- Less running around
- Less house
- Less toys
- Less everything that isn't actually essential to your daily life

- Less everything that doesn't actually bring you joy

Okay. Less is more. I've heard it before. I get it. Well, not quite.

Minimalism is not about the absence of stuff; it is about the presence of meaning and potential.

Yes, a lot of this book is about how to get rid of things, BUT the reason we're getting rid of those uncomfortable chairs that are too fancy to sit in anyway is to have more room to build forts, or finally have room for family yoga in the morning. Think of everything you could do if you didn't have to vacuum 3,000 square feet of house!

Minimalism is not just a test of will to see how long you can live without buying another pair of pants; it frees us from our commitment to the unimportant and refocuses our commitment on the people and pursuits that truly mean something to us.

TALK WITH YOUR FAMILY

I cannot stress enough how important it is to get your family on board with this.

Before you single-handedly donate everything in your house to the closest goodwill and contact the realtor to find a 500 sf. log cabin, talk to your family first.

Big lifestyle changes like this can't be made alone, and to make real changes you're going to need support and commitment from everyone. You don't want to move from a clutter-filled stressful life to a complaint-filled stressful life.

So how the heck do you get started?

CHAPTER THREE: ALL YOUR STUFF

*T*he easiest way to start is with the most visible representation of the clutter in your life: actual, physical clutter. Start with your house. Remember that your home is meant to be a place to make memories, have fun, and relax; it's not a museum, or a library, or a way to impress neighbors.

INVOLVE YOUR FAMILY

There might be some — reluctance — to getting rid of some things – particularly toys, which kids have a tendency to get emotionally attached to. But this is where a good conversation beforehand, introducing everyone to minimalism and sharing what you hope you will all gain by this is so critical. Stress that if you have less stuff, you actually have more time to play because you won't have to clean up all the time. Explain that these things are being given to other kids who don't have the money to get toys.

LISTEN

Be reasonable. You can't have the final say on everything. Everyone truly needs to be a part of the process, with the ability to make some decisions about their own possessions. Also be sure you're following your own rules. If you're keeping three hair brushes but making your spouse choose between two button-down white shirts, none of this is going to work.

WORK AT YOUR OWN PACE

Everything doesn't have to be done in a crazed flurry in one weekend (and really shouldn't be). It's just as easy to regret hastily getting rid of something as it is to regret hastily buying something. This should be a thoughtful, cathartic process – remember, you're doing this because you want to!

Have your family set a reasonable goal: one room per month, one thing per day, one drawer per week. Make a chart to go along with it (or better yet, have the kids make it!), with the goal clearly stated and check boxes for each milestone. If you think it will help, have a small reward for meeting each goal, but make sure that doesn't become the primary motivation.

IS THIS IMPORTANT TO ME? IS IT USEFUL?

Ask yourself these questions with everything you see as you begin to clear your home of the non-essential.

Be sure you're not asking yourself "Is the person who gave this to me important?" or "Is the memory associated with this important?" because the answer to those questions is probably *yes*.

I know it's one thing to say all of this, and yet when you look at the hot pink hippo that's been sitting on your dresser since your daughter gave it to you when she was four years old, all you can think is "But my daughter gave it to me!"

I totally get it.

But what is really important here? The hippo? Or the huge smile your daughter had when she saw you open that present?

Forgive me for being blunt, but your daughter might not even remember giving that to you and wonder why you've kept such a hideous hippo for so long. What matters is that she loved you then, she loves you now, and she will always love you. If you are truly afraid that the memory associated with that moment may fade if you get rid of the item, then write it in a journal; you can even take a picture of it and put it in the journal. Write down everything that that dreadful hippo represents to you, and share that with your child now; I bet you a million hugs that your son or daughter will appreciate that more than knowing that it's sitting on your dresser collecting dust.

This strategy is a good way to deal with any item that was given to you. Write a letter (Yes, a *for real* letter!) explaining what you're doing and why you're getting rid of the item, and how much it means to you that they thought of you enough to give it to you. If they're a real friend, then they'll understand and appreciate the thoughtfulness you're showing by trusting them with your honesty.

WORK CLOCKWISE

This may not work with what you're doing (it's hard to work clockwise in a drawer), but I have always cleaned this way and find it a great way to keep myself on task and organize my actions.

When you walk into a room, straight ahead of you becomes "12 o'clock;" start there, and then move right to 1 o'clock, 2 o'clock, and so on.

Working this way is very efficient because it keeps you from erratically moving from one side of the room to the other, so it's easy to tell which sections you've already combed through; it can also keep you from feeling overwhelmed when you're not sure where to start.

STAY FOCUSED

Don't let yourself get distracted. There are the obvious distractions (phone calls, needy kids), but there are also distractions that are more insidious that can occur without you recognizing them as such.

Let me explain.

You're purging your bedroom, right? So why are you downstairs putting your kids' shoes away? Why are you sitting on your bed writing in your memory journal? Yes, these things need to be done, but right now they're keeping you from completing the task at hand. Keep a bunch of bins with you wherever you are:

- one big bin one for donations
- one for recyclables
- one small bin one for trash (we borrow our planet from our grandchildren, people!)
- one for things you're donating but need to write about first
- and one for things you're keeping but belong elsewhere in the house

I know it seems like a lot, but this way you never leave the room, and you're keeping everything clearly organized so you can deal with it all after you're done.

Also, don't start choosing homes for everything you're keeping (and that is staying in the room) until you're done either. You're going to be so excited with all of the new-found room on your bureau that you'll want to start decorating immediately, but that's just another distraction!

If you want it, keep it!

Here's the deal: when you're done cleansing your home of the unimportant, no one from the **Center for Minimalism Authentication** (there is no such thing, don't worry!) is going to come to your house and inspect it.

This is something you're doing for yourself and your family, not to gain approval from other minimalists.

So, if you're looking at that hot pink hippo and saying "I actually really love this hippo. When I look at its black sunglasses with red rhinestones, and its lime green t-shirt with 'Hot Hippo' emblazoned across it, I smile and feel like all is right with the world," then for crying out loud, keep the thing! This process is not meant to be a test of your commitment to living with less. You don't have to get rid of everything in your house just to feel like you're being a "good" minimalist. If you ask yourself "Is this important to me?" and the answer is "Yes," then no matter how absolutely tacky that hippo is, keep it!

Particularly Pesky Possessions

I'm not going to go room by room and dispense ideas for every feasible item you may possibly have in your home.

Neither of us has that kind of time!

However, there are a few things that just about everyone has that deserve special attention because they usually come in great quantity and are just... well... pesky!

BOOKS

Ah, books: my Achilles' heel.
Before my daughter was born, my spouse and I were hard core book collectors; not the professional kind that look for first editions or anything like that, but the kind that frequent used book stores and buy

books because they look interesting.

Our house was filled with books – nearly every shelf had books on it.

We had probably read about half of them, which – granted – isn't a bad percentage, but it took having to redo our office as our daughter's bedroom to make us realize how much books had really taken over our house. As I went through, I realized that a lot of the books we had accumulated represented either something that we wanted to better about ourselves (John Adams because I didn't know enough about our country's history), or a sign of intelligence or cultural refinement (The Complete Works of Lewis Carroll in the living room).

One of these books was going to change me into a better person – I just had to hold on to them a little longer and I'd read them and instantly become a Renaissance Woman.

Well, there are these places... where you can get books for free... (you know where I'm going with this) called... *libraries*! And when you've finished reading Crime and Punishment and discover that it's not all it's cracked up to be, you get to give it back to the library and it's out of your house forever!!

I have to admit that it took me a while before I was comfortable with the notion that we don't have to own every great book ever written from Homer to Jhumpa Lahiri just to be able to read it. Our personal library does not represent our personal enlightenment.

The worst (and now best) part is there is a library *one mile* from our house! However, nowadays you don't even have to leave your house to borrow books from the library – an increasing number of titles are digitally available to borrow for your e-reader. Amazon.com even has a digital borrowing program for a monthly subscription fee.

PAPER

Paper is tough. It comes completely unsolicited in the mail, you get report cards, tests, and notices from your kids, and it all ends up stacked on your previously pristine kitchen island or blanketing the fridge. Here are a few strategies that you can try to minimize paper clutter:

MAIL

• Open mail right next to the shredder (for mail with confidential information such as account numbers) or recycle bin.

• Keep a basket near where you open the mail for items that need to be saved, and file or scan everything in there at least once per week.

• For junk mail, call the phone number listed on the letter and tell them to remove your address from their mailing list. Be sure to jot on a calendar the phone number you called, and the date of both when you called and when they say you should stop receiving their mail. If you get anything after that date, just call them again. There are also paid services that will reduce your junk mail for you.

• Sometimes what you think is junk mail may actually be helpful or interesting. For example, for the longest time I would immediately recycle the coupon and grocery flyers we received. But when we started keeping a more detailed budget, I realized there were actually coupons in there we could use, and knowing where the sales were helped guide my grocery shopping trips.

BILLS

• Going paperless with bills is so easy these days. Businesses don't want to have to pay postage for paper bills any more than you want them stacking up on your counter. Go to their websites or call their customer service to find out how to either get email notices or get the bills paid automatically from your bank account.

TAXES/IMPORTANT DOCUMENTS

• Some stuff you just have to save: birth certificates, social security cards, passports, etc. However, papers like tax returns, receipts, and old bank statements can be scanned and saved digitally. If you're really afraid of losing this information, make two copies of everything. Make sure everything is clearly labeled (e.g. *"Tax Returns and Supporting Documentation: 2005-2010"*).

INVITATIONS

• Write it on your calendar with a note about anything you need to bring, and take a picture of the invitation on your phone so you have all of the details. If you're really worried you'll forget, set reminders on your phone.

ACCOMPLISHMENTS/ARTWORK

• (Good grades, stick drawings of the family, etc.) Again: the scanner is our friend! Try keeping one paper per kid on the fridge; when another paper comes in that they want to post in this coveted real estate, put the other aside in a bin to be scanned (if you want). You can even make picture books of the pieces that you like the best.

Basically: scan, recycle, repeat!

CLOTHES

For women, clothes are probably one of the hardest places to purge. We're so rarely satisfied with our body shape that we hold on to clothing that doesn't fit for years by saying "I'll work out more this year. It will fit next summer."

I am *so* guilty of this. Can you say baby weight??? I gained – gulp – 60 pounds when I was pregnant, and even when I got back to my original weight, it was distributed completely differently and my pre-baby clothes still didn't fit!

CAPSULE WARDROBE

When I first started learning about minimalism, the term capsule wardrobe kept popping up. A capsule wardrobe is a collection of a small number of core pieces (dresses, pants, coats) that are all coordinated with each other, and supplemented with sets of seasonal items (shirts, accessories, leggings); the point is to be able to mix and match to create as many different outfits with as little clothing as possible.

With a capsule wardrobe, you don't have to feel so bad about getting rid of clothes that don't fit and finally breaking down and buying clothes that do, because even if you do eventually reach your "ideal" weight, your wardrobe is way smaller and you don't have to replace so much!

And as with everything minimalist, don't feel trapped. If you need more than two pairs of jeans, then keep them. However, a good way to test whether you DO actually need those "extra" clothes is to strip your wardrobe down as much as you can stand it, pack it away in bins, and see how far you get; you may be surprised by what you can get by without.

And remember, the whole point of this entire process is to free yourself from the "power" of stuff. Those size 8 pants do not represent a you that doesn't exist anymore – they're just an old pair of pants!

KIDS' CLOTHES

I certainly don't have to tell you that kids grow out of their clothing faster than we can buy them! One good idea to manage the constant need to weed out small clothes and the high volume of clothing that can accumulate if said weeding doesn't occur, is to have a basket in each kid's room for clothing that doesn't fit anymore. When your son or daughter puts something on and it's too small, it's up to them to put it in the "For Other Nice Boys/Girls" basket.

If there are clothes that your kids love and don't want to get rid of but are way past the too small point (your daughter's "Caroline Herschel is My Favorite Rock Star" t-shirt, perhaps?), cut out the graphic and sew it onto a pillowcase or a blank t-shirt that does fit.

[P.S. In case you haven't heard of her, Caroline Herschel was the first woman to discover a comet.]

PICTURES

Photographs are such powerful time capsules – a moment captured that will never come again. However, they are also very often clutter culprits.

(This is another of my soft spots: my daughter is the cutest kid ever created, so it's totally normal that I have about 1,000 pictures for every year she's been alive, right...??)

These days, pictures aren't filling our closets in shoeboxes as much as they're taking up gigabytes of storage on our various hand-held devices, computers, and hard drives. Those pictures aren't doing anyone any good locked up in this digital format. There are a bunch of websites that enable you to upload pictures and make beautiful canvas frames, collages, and books, so choose your favorites and showcase those memories, then put all of the pictures on thumb drives or CDs/DVDs and store them in a fireproof box.

The Internet is NOT a Photo Album

Before you post your next picture on social media, check the terms of service: by uploading that picture, are you granting the website full license to every picture? If you are, that means the site can use those pictures however they want, including in advertisements; they can even delete your pics if they run out of space on their server. DO NOT use a website as your primary photo storage location. Not only are those pictures and memories too important and private to be used in an energy drink ad, but you also don't want to run the risk of losing them to a website crash or hacker.

TOYS & GIFTS

If you assess all of the toys in your home, I'll bet that about half of them were given to your children by friends and family for their birthdays or other holidays; this is where telling family and friends that your family is going minimalist will be crucial. Make the purging process as public as you can: go ahead and share before and after pictures online, go ahead and post how excited you were when your spouse found a local charity that takes both toys and toasters. You want everyone to know what you're doing and why, because not only will this hopefully inspire others to follow your lead, but it will also make them think twice about buying you and the kids things that you don't really need or want.

But gifts from others mean that they were thinking of you, right?

Well, yes... but only if it's something that truly reflects your personality. People are often hungry for some sort of direction and guidance regarding gift-giving, but they're too timid to ask because they think that means they don't know you well enough. If you're an eco-conscious global citizen, talk to your mother-in-law (or better yet, have your spouse talk to her!) about your values and the kinds of things you want to bring into your home BEFORE she buys your 6-month-old a neon pink plastic teething ring that was manufactured 10,000 miles away.

To get in front of unwanted birthday gifts, include a wish list with party invitations – nothing too specific (this isn't a wedding registry), but more like "wooden toys, thrift store gift cards, starter cello." Remember to be grateful even if you get a present that doesn't fit your new lifestyle. Not everyone will understand, and they are trying to express their love in their way.

Same deal for other holidays: if you know of certain items that would be helpful for you or your family, then create wish lists and send them out to family and friends well in advance of the holiday. Invite others to reciprocate with their own lists. Or, if you really can't think of any thing that would be useful, suggest charities people can donate to, or activities you'd like to do with people for your gift. People want to give you a gift that is meaningful, useful, and memorable – they might just need a little help figuring out what that is!

GARBAGE

Think about all of the garbage that goes out of your house every week. When you're a minimalist, you start seeing excess everywhere – even product packaging. Next time you go shopping for groceries or household items, look at the packaging: is it wrapped in three layers of plastic and cardboard? If so, do some research to see if you can find the same item but in larger quantity so less packaging is used; if that doesn't work, see if there is a comparable alternative at another store or online. Also, write (yes, a *for real* letter – mail is way more noticeable and effective these days than email) to the manufacturer of the item and tell them why you're considering switching. The power of the pocketbook is real, and not only will you reduce the amount of waste leaving your home, you could help persuade an international company to change its ways, thus reducing waste at a global level: a minimalist's dream come true!!

KEEP YOUR EYES OPEN

There is likely clutter in places that you don't even see anymore: magnets on the fridge, pictures on the walls, spatulas, pencils, etc. Now that your sixth minimalist sense has been activated, you'll be sniffing out clutter in all kinds of unexpected places!

DON'T FORGET THE YARD

Once you've conquered the interior of your house, turn your attention to the exterior. You don't have to become a master Bonsai gardener to be a minimalist – just think about all of the creative ways you can apply the principles of simplicity and balance to your yard. The goal here is the same as it was with the inside of your house: ask yourself what you need and what you enjoy. Are your kids too big for the jungle gym? Do you dread the spring because that means you have to clean and reopen the pool? Does anyone even swim in the pool anymore? Do you really love all of those garden gnomes and silhouetted cowboys? If it's not important to you or useful, you know what to do.

 Consider starting a garden. Gardens are a perfect way to involve your family: bring them with you to the nursery to help pick out plants, let them help plant the seeds, water the garden, weed, and harvest (if you're growing food). If you're feeling particularly ambitious, ask each of your kids to pick a color and only select plants of those colors. My sister had a great idea to plant sunflowers and took pictures of her 4-year-old next to them every week or so – what a difference between week 1 and week 10!

HOW DO I GET RID OF ALL THIS STUFF?!?

Sell

There are SO MANY websites now dedicated to helping you get rid of your stuff: eBay, Craigslist, and even Amazon are just the tip of the iceberg. AbeBooks, PaperbackSwap (and its sister sites CDSwap and DVDSwap), Freecycle, and so many others will either pay you directly or provide you with a means of bartering your stuff away. And of course there's always the good old fashioned yard sale that never goes out of style.

Donate

Again, there are countless charities and thrift stores that will gladly accept your used possessions, ranging from computers to junk cars to car seats; just please follow their guidelines and donate truly usable items. Don't take advantage of the charity's good deed by donating a box full of broken electronics or scratched CDs. It's also a good idea to do a little bit of research on the charity you're considering donating to. Sites like CharityNavigator.com evaluate charities on a number of factors, helping to make sure that it's a reputable and responsible organization.

Recycle

Some stuff is just hard to get rid of: fluorescent light bulbs, batteries, paint, broken small appliances, etc. First step is to call your town hall and see if there are any town programs. Be patient; some cities and towns may only accept certain items at specific times of year, but it's worth it to dispose of these things properly and safely (the planet you save could be your own!).

If that doesn't work, call around to local churches, schools, and charities; these organizations will sometimes run collection drives. Some stores will also accept such items for recycling. Be sure to ask whoever is going to take these items if there is a fee.

If you can't find a local recipient, there are some websites that will help you get rid of these problem items, although you're likely going to have to pay for the shipping, which can be exorbitant depending on the item. Also, ask if these items will be shipped and recycled overseas, as American companies are required to follow more rigorous environmental and labor regulations when it comes to this type of waste.

ONE IN, ONE OUT!

After you load up the car (and the other car... and your friends' cars...) and get all of that stuff out of your house, set a rule: one in, one out. This can be applied as broadly or as specifically as you like: for some, it's just a way to manage kids' toys; for others, anyone who brings something into the house to stay means they have to pick something else of theirs to go. This rule is a great way to keep your home clutter-free.

Now that your home is owned by you and not your stuff, let's talk about less tangible (but equally as obtrusive) clutter...

CHAPTER FOUR: SPENDING
YOUR TIME & MONEY WISELY

*T*hink about what you spend your time doing on a daily basis, and ask yourself the same questions as you did when you were evaluating your possessions: "What is important to me? What is useful?" Do you really believe in the missions of all six of the committees you're on, OR were you pressured or guilt-tripped into joining some of those?

How about all of the time you spend...

- *cleaning*

- *driving to and from parties, errands, and stores*

- *reading about or watching other people's lives on social media or TV*

- *looking for your keys, your spouse's glasses, or your kid's sneakers*

Imagine spending all of that time working on your family scrapbook, or volunteering, or finally going to that hot yoga class, or skydiving, or... ANYTHING ELSE you actually want to do!!

Time is our most precious possession, especially for us moms who watch our kids change from helpless squirming spit-up machines to physics majors in what seems like a matter of minutes!

[In fact, I value your time so much I would like to THANK YOU AGAIN for reading this book!]

By employing the principles of minimalism, we adjust our daily routines to revolve around what is important and useful, achieving a balance between all of the different facets of our lives.

WORKING IN AN OFFICE

When you're in the office, you're either working, looking for information and/or things, or talking to people. Do you spend too much of your time on the last two and not enough on the first? If so, think of ways you can apply the minimalist guidelines here to save you time and stress:

• Instead of doing everything yourself, delegate time-intensive research and some of your other more menial tasks.

• If your office is cluttered with furniture, paper, office supplies, take a day to purge and reorganize; if you have to do this during the weekend because your work is too busy, rope the family into helping, or at least make them visit you for a picnic in the office.

• Get rid of any files in your office that aren't directly relevant to your current projects.

• If you're constantly interrupted with questions from coworkers, place a "Can we chat later?" note on your door or cubicle.

• Beware of desktop "organizers," meaning all of those paper and folder holders that sit on your desk or filing cabinet and are really just clutter holders. Sometimes people think that all they need to get organized is another stackable paper tray, when in fact they're just making room for stuff they don't need.

WORKING FROM HOME

It can be particularly challenging finding balance between work and home when there is no physical barrier between the two. It's so easy to get dragged into an email exchange when you hear the alert on your phone and all you have to do is hit a couple buttons and it's done. The problem is that we teach people how to treat us, and if your coworkers or clients see you working at all hours, then they're going to assume it's okay to call you at all hours. Make it clear to people when you're available and – more importantly – when you're not, and stick to that schedule.

While your coworkers and clients need your attention during work hours, your family deserves 100% of your attention the rest of the time. Don't check work email during dinner. Don't answer your phone during your son's volleyball game.

If your family starts to feel sidelined, they'll start getting your attention in other less enjoyable ways (can you say temper tantrums and slammed doors...?). If you're honest with yourself, you probably know whether you cut into family time too often, but talk to your family anyway and ask them whether they think you need to be more present with them.

ANOTHER CAREER PATH...?

Another more difficult question to ask yourself is whether you actually enjoy your work, or if you're only doing it for a sense of security or pride. Soon after our daughter was born, I realized that what I really wanted was to stay home and focus entirely on her development and our relationship. Luckily, when I crunched the numbers I discovered that we could get by on one income if we tightened our belts a bit.

However, the biggest hurdle I had to get past was linking my self-respect (and my spouse's respect for me) with having my own income. Every day for a month I asked myself "Is my job important to me?" and I found myself saying "No" way more than "Yes."

I'm not trying to make everyone reading this a SAHM (*Stay At Home Mom*). I'm just pointing out that you need to ask yourself the question.

Maybe you don't want to be a SAHM but you would like a career change. Maybe the commute is cutting too much into family time. Obviously, sometimes our financial situation is more restrictive than we'd like, so of course providing for our families is our foremost responsibility; just make sure your job isn't weighing you down mentally, spiritually, or physically.

§

Cleaning

The Good News: with far less stuff in the house, cleaning is going to be *way easier*!!

The Bad News: we still have to clean.

Division of labor is critical here – make sure you're not doing everything yourself! Minimalism requires BALANCE: a balanced mind, a balanced life, and a balanced workload. Sit with your family and make a list of all of the chores that have to be done on a weekly and monthly basis, then figure out a rotation schedule. Remember not to criticize how someone does a chore, as long as they tried their best. If you tell your son that he never fills the dishwasher the right way, he's just going to refuse to do it next time.

Include your spouse in this too: according to a study conducted by the University of British Columbia, fathers who equally divided household chores with their wives tended to have daughters whose career aspirations were less gender-stereotypical. Your daughter could discover the key to long-term space travel if your husband would just fold the laundry!

Just accept it...

...the house is never going to be as clean as we want it to be... but where's the fun in living in a completely pristine house anyway? Generally, taking 30 minutes to an hour each day to clean is plenty of time to keep the house in acceptable and livable condition. Taking your shoes off inside the door is also a great way to limit the amount of outside crud that infiltrates your clean floors; make sure you have slippers for guests with cold feet though!

CLEANING SUPPLY CLUTTER

How many bottles of multi-purpose cleaner do you really need, anyway (especially when vinegar and water is the best cleaner ever created)? If you have a closet full of cleaning supplies that you don't think you'll ever use, ask friends and family if they want any of them. Don't donate open bottles, but if you have any unopened bottles, feel free to pay those forward.

If you can't pawn those cleaning supplies off on anyone else, bite the bullet and just use them. Pick a bottle and make that your go-to cleaner until it's gone, and keep going until they're all gone... then go buy more vinegar and baking soda!

ৡ

COOKING

Are you the type of mom who feels guilty if every dinner isn't a grand, four-course affair? Perhaps you're the type who forgets about dinner until your spouse is pulling in the driveway and you reach for the frozen pizza for the·third time that week? Unless you love to cook, meals can feel like a huge burden: we want to give our families tasty and nutritious food, but we don't want to spend hours preparing a lavish meal just to see it devoured thanklessly in ten minutes either.

Think about the way meals are prepared in your home and how you can better balance and manage this continuous task:

• Switch it Up. If your kids are old enough, and if your spouse is home early enough, have them each take on a night to make dinner. If you want to make it particularly challenging, make a rule that no frozen foods are allowed.

• Get Help. If your kids are not old enough to handle cooking a meal on their own, then make them participate in age-appropriate ways like measuring, stirring, chopping, or setting the table.

• Let Others Have A Say. You don't have to come up with meal ideas all on your own. Have each family member propose as many meal choices as they want for the week, and involve them in the shopping and preparation for those meals.

• Prepare Ingredients Early. If you know you're going to have salad every day, then chop some of the vegetables right when you bring them home from the grocery store; this dramatically reduces prep time during the week. You can even make some meals days early and freeze them if you know it's going to be a particularly hectic week.

Again, our goal here is to reduce stress associated with cooking and make family meals more enjoyable and balanced.

GROCERY SHOPPING

Spending less time grocery shopping means more time spent on more important activities. We've all heard the advice: make a list and stick to it, buy in bulk, make a menu for the week, etc., and a lot of it is incredibly useful and logical. However, make sure that all of those "money-saving" tips are actually helping you and your family achieve a more balanced schedule and budget.

Bulk shopping, for example, may make a lot of sense for some people, but do the savings really make up for the membership fee or the long drive?

When I was first thinking about quitting my job, I saw our grocery budget as the perfect place to shed some expenses, and I set about analyzing and comparing the prices of all of the grocery stores in our area. I spent hours going to each store, dragging our daughter through every aisle so I could comb the shelves for the items we buy on a regular basis, writing down prices and package sizes so I could compare per unit costs, calculating the cost of gas to go to each store, and entering all of this data into my Groceries Analysis spreadsheet.

I'm not kidding.

I did this.

For real.

And you know what I discovered? It really didn't make much of a difference where I shopped – all of them were pretty comparable. Driving to three different stores each week just to get the best deal on organic peanut butter or use the coupon for laundry detergent was A) not worth the gas, and B) not worth the time.

I'm glad that I did it, because now I know.

But in actuality, the biggest impact that we made on our food budget was finding creative ways to eat the food that was already in our house instead of buying more to make our standard go-to meals. We didn't realize we had so much food in our house until I discovered we were already over-budget on the 21st of the month!

MINIMIZE YOUR FOOD'S FOOTPRINT

Minimalism is not just about finding balance within yourself and your own family, but with your environment as well. Look at the food in your house and think about the distances everything had to travel, or the chemical preservatives used to keep that strawberry looking red for a month. Local, organic food is the best way to feed your family.

You may balk at the price at the grocery store when you compare it to non-organic food, but buying direct at farmers' markets are usually way more reasonable. Plus, the low price of that pesticide-laden food does not include the toll on your family's (and the farmer's) long-term health, or the cost of manually pollinating food when all of the bees are gone, or the toll on biodiversity when species are going extinct due to habitat loss so we can try to grow another 100 acres of palm trees in the rainforest.

Is it really important that you buy peaches from China in February? Or can you wait until June or July when they're in season in your area and have a fun weekend with the family picking and canning? Showing your children where food actually comes from and cultivating a stronger connection to their food is an invaluable tool in educating them to respect and love their environment.

FAMILY AND FRIENDS

Do Nothing This Weekend

A strong network of family and friends is critical to happiness and a balanced life, but having every weekend filled for the next three months with birthday parties, weddings, sports events, etc. can be stressful. First of all, make sure it's important for you to attend all of these activities: your nephew's 16th birthday? Probably. Your cousin's third lacrosse game of the season? Probably not.

Have your family pick an upcoming weekend during which you will all stay home and do nothing together. Maybe a family movie marathon day is just what you all need. Or a day of playing in the pool, or doing crafts. Keep the phones on silent. Don't check your email or social media. The goal of this (in)activity is to relax, enjoy being with each other, and appreciate your comfortable home.

Social Media

Social networking sites can be a great way to stay in touch with friends and family. However, they can also be a huge time suck if you let them.

Don't worry about missing out on the latest funny video clip or picture

– it will be on the internet FOREVER!! Is it really important that you read and comment on every one of your friends' posts? Or are you doing it because you want to feel included? Or maybe you're worried that someone will be offended if you don't respond within a few minutes?

Think about what this kind of behavior is teaching our children about friendships and how to be a real friend. Actual friendships are based on helping each other, shared memories, and compatible personalities. If someone is really your friend, then you don't have to worry about immediately seeing their vacation pictures or their rant about cheese snobs – you guys will talk about it next time you see each other! The less time you spend commenting online, the more time you can spend in your friends' company making new memories.

Party Planning

Kids' parties – birthday parties in particular – have become the new battle ground for "keeping up with the Joneses." Party themes, invitations, activities, goodie bags, and cake designs have somehow become the basis on  which other parents judge how creative you are and how much you love your kids. And it's hard not to feel inadequate when the last party your son went to had a bouncy house, a three-tier flaming cake, and an entire petting zoo.

Think about your child and what he or she actually enjoys, and base your party around that. Parties don't have to be expensive, ornate affairs to be fun. The truth is that a good treasure map with fun clues and hidden goodies all over the house and yard will keep kids entertained for a long time.

KEEPING A BUDGET

Your expenses are another great place to trim excess. But before you can start eliminating or reducing bills, you need to make sure you have a clear picture of all of the money coming in and where it's going.

I'm not going to get into all of the various ways you can track and manage your spending – there is plenty of useful information out there from really smart financial advisors and experts. But what I will say is don't get bogged down in all of the advice, apps, and spreadsheets. Find a system that works for you and stick to it.

Once you have a better understanding of your spending habits, put on your minimalist goggles and remember our mantra: "Is this important? Is this useful?" Do you need 600 TV channels, plus Hulu and Netflix subscriptions? Do  you need to go out to eat every week? Will you really be that uncomfortable if you lower the thermostat three degrees and put on a sweater?

This is another perfect time to involve the family. Discuss how everyone can contribute to lowering the monthly expenses, as well as what your family would like to do with the savings. How about a family vacation? Figure out how much that vacation costs, have everyone help make a fun "Countdown to Kennedy Space Center" sign, and track your progress.

PAYING OFF DEBT

We've all heard the staggering statistics about families with credit card debt and student loan debt. Living simply with a minimalist mindset is a great way to have a direct impact on your finances.

Cut up those credit cards! Consolidate those loans! Sell that car with the high loan and insurance payments! Spending less on the unnecessary frees your money to have a greater impact on eliminating those interminable monthly payments.

CASH OR CREDIT?

There are a lot of financial gurus out there touting the power of cash, and I agree. Paying with cash is an entirely different feeling than paying with a card, and reducing the number of credit cards you have is another fine way to live minimally.

However, using a credit card can be a good thing if you're selective about it. For example, some stores give you a discount off your entire purchase every time you use their card. If their prices are reasonable for what you already buy, AND you trust yourself not to shop there more often just because you have a card there, then consider getting a card. DON'T sign up for a store card just to get a promotional one-time discount for signing up – it's not worth it unless there is a consistent discount and you already shop there often.

A lot of major credit cards also give you cash back rewards, but make sure the fine print doesn't make it impossible to ever get that reward due to a myriad of restrictions or absurd payout minimums.

As always, before you buy anything, ask yourself those two questions you've now gotten tattooed on your forearms: "Is it important? Is it useful?"

Now it's time for you and your family to...

Get Started!

YOU CAN DO THIS!! All of that stuff and stress has no power over you anymore!

Go get your family as excited as you are about giving to others, cleaning less, and going on longer vacations! Teach your kids to value people, time, and experiences more than things, invitations, and "Likes."

Teach your family to love the questions "Is this important? Is this useful?" as much as you do and start living with MORE!

You're going to have so much *roooom* in your life, you will even have time for that massage...

GOOD
LUCK!

YOUR OPINION

Did you like *Minimalism For Moms*? The book to help you *Simplify, Declutter, and Organize Your Way to a Stress-Free and Meaningful Life*?

If you enjoyed reading this book, I would love it if you would help others enjoy it as well. **LEND** it, **RECOMMEND** it, or **REVIEW** it.

You can help other readers find this book by recommending it to friends and family in person and on social media, in reading and discussion groups, on online forums, or other sites. You can also review it on the site where you purchased it. If you do happen to write a review, please inform me via an email to *rachelhathawaywriter@gmail.com*, and I'll thank you with a personal email.

ABOUT THE AUTHOR

Rachel Hathaway is the pen name for a professional writer whom you may or may not know (Mysterious, huh?). Her work spans many areas of creative fiction -- including the very wide romance genre -- as well as her published non-fiction self-help guides, personal growth and development ebooks, and a large number of articles and posts across the web on a variety of sites and blogs about smart modern shopping, style, music, the arts, and a range of eco-friendly topics. She lives in New England with her *devoted* in their dream home, and they make sure to enjoy the wonderful aspects of life on a daily basis.

Published by RH Media.

UPDATED

Paleo

Diet

FOOD

LiST

Rachel Hathaway

Published by RH Media. v. 1.5
Also available in paperback (English), and in Spanish ebook and paperback editions

*** Also available in audiobook ***

FEEDBACK

ACTUAL READER REVIEWS OF THIS BOOK

***** (FIVE STARS) EXACTLY WHAT I WAS LOOKING FOR!

"I previously purchased a beginners guide to the paleo diet that did not have list of foods. This book is an excellent reference guide!"

***** (FIVE STARS) DIET FOOD LIST

"This is my kind of "diet" book. All I want to know is what I should / should not eat. I don't follow recipes, so just give me the ingredients and let me go at it. No more sifting though all those boring pages of drivel that only help me lose weight because I'm sitting down... and hopefully not snacking while I'm reading. The author's carefree, fun style makes this an even more enjoyable read."

**** (FOUR STARS) EASY WAY

"It does as it says and cuts to the chase of what one should eat on this diet."

PREFACE

Here's your **Updated Paleo Diet Food List** (with a few choice sample shopping lists!)

Start making healthy paleo breakfast, lunch, and dinner today! Your simple guide to easy Paleo shopping is all about finding the right ingredients: GET THIS BOOK BEFORE YOU STOCK UP ON TOO MANY PALEO RECIPE BOOKS... WHY? Have you ever wanted a quick idea of what's on and off the shopping list for a Paleo diet? This paleo diet for beginners book provides a fun way to navigate through the grocery store, the restaurant menu, or your kitchen cabinets and fridge.

Here's your useful list -- by category -- of suggested and acceptable:

- meats,
- veggies,
- fruits,
- fish,
- nuts,
- oils,
- and more -- *everything you need to go PALEO!*

PREPARE GREAT PALEO MEALS

Whether you're making healthy paleo smoothies for breakfast, paleo Mexican for lunch, asian paleo for dinner, or just trying to figure out what to put in your slow cooker, it all comes down to the very BEST INGREDIENTS! When you're too busy to go out to the store every time you find a great paleo recipe, you won't be able to benefit from the consistency of maintaining this Stone Age, hunter-gatherer diet. Having this UPDATED PALEO DIET FOOD LIST BOOK means that your fridge, your cabinets, and you pantry will always be ready to go caveman, cavegirl, and paleolithic! ROCK ON with this book!!!

INTRODUCTION

Thanks for checking out my new book! When my Mom, who has tried every diet under the sun, told me that she was switching to a Paleo Diet and having some early success, I immediately asked her what she can eat.

I thought it was a simple question.

I guess I was wrong...

She had a vague answer about "hunter/gatherers" and how it was probably the very first human diet. She said she had heard that the diet of most Americans/Europeans consists of about 70% processed foods. But when it came right down to it, she wasn't all that sure about the specifics of the plan.

After telling me some weird story about old stone tools, and then digressing about the weather in her part of the country, she mentioned a few recipes books that she had tried and started rattling off some of the ingredients in those.

"Not super helpful, Mom."

"Why?" she asked.

So I told her, "Mom, this is what I need: I need an absolutely useable food list for a Paleo diet!"

And, more importantly, I wanted to know which foods to avoid.

I wanted to know straight away, not through a series of disconnected recipes…

And then after doing a bunch of research with the staffers at RH Media, we came up with this newly UPDATED PALEO FOOD LIST, and the very first copy will go to my Mom!

(Let's call it a late/early Mother's Day gift!)

Why?

It's fine to follow a new (old) diet, especially one that seems to be working for you, but recipes can be sort of limiting.

I want to know what to buy, what I should eat when I'm at home, and what I'm able to eat when I go to a restaurant. I need to plan meals for the week, or I won't really stick to ANY plan. I know myself too well. I have shelves of great recipe books, and the photos are spectacular, but I can count on one hand how many of those recipes I've made.

I can't constantly cross-reference Paleo diet breakfast, lunch, and dinner recipes to build a series of meals, especially my lunches for work. I want to have a good idea now of what's likely IN and what's OUT with this diet.

And when I see online that Paleo can still work vegan at times (we try once a week), and I can still fire up the slow cooker, I want to know how.

WHAT THIS BOOK IS AND WHAT IT ISN'T

First of all, this book is not some blanket endorsement of a Paleo diet. I'm not really sure how well it works YET, and whatever I've heard is just chatter among some of my peeps.

Enough said.

So that means you need to make up your own mind if a Paleo diet plan even makes sense for you. (You should probably also consult your doctor or other medical professional before you make changes to your diet anyway. That's what I try to do.) I don't know if I'll lose weight, look great in my bathing suit, or have a lot more energy, but I do know I need this list!!

After that, please understand that there are no recipes here. This is a book about possibilities, and actually helps me more than flipping through a number of possibly tasty recipes, all the while keeping an eye on the estimated PREP time. Personally, I look down these lists here and see hundreds of recipes between the lines.

I just want a PALEO FOOD LIST to have a quick look at the ingredients that I should watch for at the store, and, according to this plan, things I should probably skip. And since I can have this ebook on my smartphone, problem solved!

Simple, huh?

That's the beauty of this. Hopefully, you'll agree.

So let's get started.

FRESH FRUITS & VEGETABLES

*S*o when it comes to vegetables in a Paleo diet, you're pretty much smooth sailing. This is why it's still totally possible to have our once-a-week vegan nights. The only thing to watch out for is legumes, starchy vegetables like potatoes, and high-sugar fruits like bananas, which aren't that good for you on any diet plan.

If you keep an eye out for some of these fruits and veggies on your next shopping trip, you can add a lot of great new flavors to your menus. (I made a point to get some cauliflower, a mango, and a bag of limes on a recent outing, and added some real variety to our week!) So here you go:

PALEO FRUIT & VEGETABLE LIST

- Apples
- Apricots
- Artichoke Hearts
- Asparagus
- Avocados
- Bananas (in moderation)
- Beets
- Blackberries
- Blueberries
- Broccoli
- Brussel Sprouts
- Cabbage
- Cantaloupe
- Carrots
- Cauliflower
- Celery
- Cherries
- Collard Greens
- Cranberries
- Cucumber
- Eggplant
- Endive
- Figs
- Grapefruit
- Grapes
- Green Onions
- Guava
- Kale
- Kiwi
- Lemons
- Limes
- Lychee

- Mangoes
- Mushrooms
- Mustard Greens
- Olives
- Oranges
- Papaya
- Parsley
- Parsnip
- Passion Fruit
- Peaches
- Pears
- Peppers (red, green, yellow)
- Persimmon
- Pineapple
- Plums
- Pomegranate
- Pumpkin
- Raspberries
- Romaine Lettuce
- Rhubarb
- Rutabaga
- Seaweed (kelp)
- Snow Peas
- Spinach
- Sprouts
- Squash
- Star Fruit
- Strawberries
- Swiss Chard
- Tangerines
- Turnips
- Watercress
- Watermelon
- Zucchini

As with many other contemporary diets, raw fruits and vegetables are pretty good for your overall energy level. I also like to drop a bunch of these fruits and veggies together into my blender/juicer machine and try to make a WOWSER drink in the morning, but raw is still the best! (Yes, I use "wowser" as a sort of technical term for really good, just go with it.)

With the right blender-bullet thingy (you know the one!), we can also grind up all of the skins, nuts, and oils we want as well. I feel better about this process than what we did with our old juicer, where it felt we were wasting so many nutritional parts of the fruits and veggies. (We've recently made some crazy-fun PALEO smoothies for example with plums, strawberries, a little spinach, a spot of olive oil, and some pumpkin seeds… it's actually really delicious as long as you use enough strawberries!)

So, as I told my Mom (and everyone else in my world!), this raw fruits/veggies thing is, OF COURSE, the perfect argument for buying organically grown fruits and veggies. Sure they wash everything, we wash everything (twice!), but if you're going to be chomping on raw stuff, isn't it better to know that it didn't have any artificial pesticides on them at any point?

We think it's totally worth it to buy organic, and since every store seems to be getting on the bandwagon of increased food safety, it's easier to find a huge variety of stuff. Plus if we all buy organic, which was the old-fashioned way before they invented all of these crazy pesticides, then the prices will have to come down. Okay Mom, I'll get off my soap box.

Next, to the meat category...

MEATS

*O*f course with a Paleo diet you need to stay away from processed meats like salami, bologna, hot dogs, and other deli wonders, but that still leaves room for a lot of other choices.

A lot. Quite.

Because of the nature of the Paleolithic diet though, a fair amount of the things you can eat in the meat category are downright strange and impractical. My Mom and her (third) husband live in the South so maybe they can find some of this stuff (doubt it!), but in New England my sweetie and I wouldn't even know where to start.

Be on the lookout for grass-fed and/or free range meat by the way, which is what you usually get when you ask for organic meat. It might take an extra detour on your way home from work, but it's worth it. (The image on our book cover is also a subtle reminder...)

PALEO MEAT LIST

- Bacon (in moderation)
- Bear
- Beef Jerky
- Bison
- Bison Jerky
- Bison Ribeye
- Bison Sirloin
- Bison Steaks
- Buffalo
- Chicken Breast (free range)
- Chicken Thighs (free range)
- Chuck Steak
- Elk
- Emu
- Goat
- Goose
- Ground Beef (free range)

- Kangaroo
- Lamb Rack
- Lean Veal
- New York Steak
- Ostrich
- Pheasant
- Poultry (above)
- Pork
- Pork Chops
- Pork Tenderloin
- Quail
- Rabbit
- Rattlesnake
- Reindeer
- Steak (above)
- Turkey
- Turtle
- Veal
- Venison Steaks
- Wild Boar

Okay seriously, I can't imagine eating bear, emu, kangaroo, ostrich, or rattlesnake, but that's me. I get a little snooty when the WIFI is down for more than fifteen minutes, so just thinking about those "meats" makes me feel WAY too rustic. And as for reindeer, I can't go there either. Too many holiday decorations bouncing around in my head, I guess. But after getting this all together, now I know why people keep mentioning bison burgers.

If you simply choose one to start with — like turkey, for example — you'll find that you're approach to preparing the meals is too limited. Forget about a single favorite recipe, family expectations, or any of that. Start from scratch. Look at these ingredients and think about the range of amazing ways you can prepare dinners for your table.

I take the same approach with everything on this list — within reason. It's lead me to reevaluate the way we prepare beef, pork, veal, steak, and more.

But now you know the full monty, Mom (and all my other wonderful readers)! But seriously, good luck finding wild boar at your local deli or supermarket.

So, let's take a look at the fish and seafood list now…

FISH & SEAFOOD

ish and a wide range of seafood and shellfish are abundant on the Paleo list. That's good because of the protein and the magic of Omega 3's. We were very happy to discover a collection of easy to find, tasty fresh and salt-water fish, and enough other choices for those special occasions.

PALEO FISH & SEAFOOD LIST

- Bass
- Clams

- Crab
- Crawfish
- Crayfish
- Halibut
- Lobster
- Mackerel
- Oysters
- Red Snapper
- Salmon
- Sardines
- Scallops
- Shark
- Shrimp
- Sole
- Sunfish
- Swordfish
- Tilapia
- Trout
- Tuna
- Wallete

For me, this list has been very helpful when we go out to eat. Swordfish, cooked in olive oil, served with lemon and garnished with parsley was something I was able to get on our last trip into the big city. (Protein and vegetables, low salt — that's always my restaurant plan these days.)

That was my first attempt to see how possible it was to follow a Paleo diet on the go!

Nailed it. (But, I'm not trying shark, though. Ever.)

Eggs are up next.

EGGS

*F*or eggs, I was glad to know that they're on the list.

What to look for:

PALEO EGG LIST

- Chicken eggs
- Duck eggs
- Goose eggs

If you can find a local farm and get some of these as free range, pastured, or organic, it's always worth it because I think the eggs are just plain better. The large goose and duck eggs are a must-have in our household now.

Pretty straightforward, huh.

Next up...

NUTS & SEEDS

I love nuts, seeds, and all manner of trail mix. After ditching processed foods, trail mix has become our snack of choice.

But honestly I had always been suspicious of nuts and seeds because they tasted so good. I know they have lots of protein, BUT they can also be high in fat.

Paleo diets suggest skipping peanuts (a legume, right!) and cashews, but the rest of these should really make for tasty snacks, and don't forget to use them as integral cooking ingredients.

PALEO NUTS & SEEDS LIST

- Almonds
- Cashews
- Hazelnuts
- Macadamia Nuts
- Pecans
- Pine Nuts
- Pumpkin Seeds
- Sunflower Seeds
- Walnuts

Of course, when I purchase these, I always look for the unsalted variety.

Next up, this brings us to healthy oils...

HEALTHY OILS & FATS

J still haven't been able to find the first one on this oils list, but I'm still looking!

This is a list of healthy oils and fats that shows up on almost everyone's "USE INSTEAD" lists! It's funny that Paleo confirms many of the things we see elsewhere about these oils.

PALEO HEALTHY OILS & FATS LIST

- Avocado Oil
- Butter (grass fed)
- Coconut Oil

- Macadamia Oil
- Olive Oil

Our staff found online that there's an interesting connection to this type of diet, without salt and processed foods, to acne. High protein diets with these oils are apparently reopening studies around the globe of connections between diet and acne, since the skin reflects what's going on in the body.

That's cool, although I'm way past my acne years... that ship has sailed.

NEXT UP:

The long-awaited "foods I should not eat, seriously avoid, or at least handle with care on my Paleo-inspired diet..."

FOOD TO AVOID ON A
PALEO DIET

*I*f you need an ANTI-SHOPPING grocery list for your Paleo diet, here it is.

I asked my Mom what stuff I should NOT buy at all of the very cool food stores near where I live, and she was stumped. Coming up with this info seems to be the most perplexing part for most new people on the Paleo diet.

As I mentioned before, this is a combination DO NOT EAT, TRY TO AVOID, or at least HANDLE WITH CARE list. In the real world, having an english muffin isn't grounds for a court-martial.

But to get the full impact of a Paleo-inspired diet, don't plan on eating or drinking these items:

PALEO AVOID LIST

- Acorn squash
- Beans (adzuki, black, broad, fava, garbanzo, green, kidney, lima, mung, navy, pinto, red, string, white)
- Beer or hard alcohol
- Beets
- Bread/Toast
- Butter (unless it's grass fed)
- Butternut squash
- Candy/junk food
- Cereal Grains
- Cheese
- Corn
- Corn syrup
- Cottage Cheese
- Crackers
- Cream Cheese
- Doughnuts
- English Muffins
- Hash Browns
- High Sugar/Fructose Fruit Juices (apple, chinola, grape, mango, orange, starfruit, or strawberry)
- Hot Dogs
- Ice Cream
- Ice Milk
- French Fries
- Frozen Yogurt
- Ketchup
- Legumes
- Lentils
- Milk (skim, 2%, low fat, or whole milk)
- Miso

- Non-fat Dairy Creamer
- Oatmeal
- Pancakes
- Pasta (all types including lasagna, spaghetti, rigatoni, and fettuccini)
- Peas (black-eyed, chickpeas, snow peas, snap peas)
- Peanuts
- Peanut Butter
- Potatoes
- Powdered Milk
- Processed Foods (chips, cookies, pastries, or pretzels)
- Refined Sugar (and artificial sweeteners)
- Reined Vegetable Oils
- Salt
- Soda or Energy Drinks
- Soybeans (and soybean products)
- Spam
- Sweet Potatoes
- Wheat
- Yams
- Yogurt
- Yucca

Of course, I could have listed SEVERAL hundred brand-name products by name, but I figure you get the idea. Much of our cabinets were overflowing with all manner of cookies, snacks, pretzels, and chips. Candy is obvious, and we made a deal to finish the ice cream in the freezer before we adopted the plan. (I don't like to waste food!)

I understand it may take some serious changes for you to enforce this type of list, but if we can manage it in our house, yours should be a SNAP!

PALEO DIET FOOD SHOPPING LIST SAMPLES

So those lists should help you at the grocery store, but I put together a few specific shopping lists that might inspire you to eat better. Again, since there aren't any recipes here, this is about seeing the possibilities in a list of wonderful, fresh, raw ingredients. I tend to improvise in the kitchen anyway. (I must have been a jazz singer in a past life!)

And as I mentioned before, try to find as many of these as you can in their USDA certified organic varieties. I think they taste better and we're still going for critical mass on lowering the cost, folks!

So let's take a look:

SAMPLE PALEO SHOPPING LIST - NUMBER ONE

1. Green Apples (organic)
2. Celery (organic)
3. Avocado (organic)

4. Eggplant (organic)
5. Green Onions (organic)
6. Coconut Oil
7. Free-range Chicken Thighs/Breasts
8. New York Steak
9. Fresh Tuna
10. Walnuts
11. Chicken Eggs (free range; organic)

SAMPLE PALEO SHOPPING LIST - NUMBER TWO

1. Artichoke hearts (organic)
2. Cabbage (organic)
3. Carrots (organic)
4. Cherries (organic)
5. Peaches (organic)
6. Red and Yellow Peppers (organic)
7. Olive Oil (organic)
8. Pork Tenderloin
9. Ground beef (free range)
10. Chicken Breast (free range)
11. Lean Veal
12. Halibut
13. Shrimp
14. Pumpkin Seeds
15. Pecans
16. Duck or Goose Eggs (free range; organic)

SAMPLE PALEO SHOPPING LIST - NUMBER THREE

1. Blueberries (organic)
2. Grapes (organic)
3. Oranges (organic)
4. Spinach (organic)
5. Cauliflower (organic)
6. Green Peppers (organic)
7. Parsley (organic)
8. Zucchini (organic)
9. Avocado Oil (organic)
10. Pork Chops
11. Beef Jerky
12. Bison Steaks
13. Chicken Thighs (free range)
14. Turkey
15. Crab
16. Scallops
17. Lobster
18. Hazelnuts
19. Sunflower Seeds
20. Pine Nuts
21. Duck or Goose Eggs (free range; organic)

❧

I hope these sample shopping lists inspire you to become a better, healthier shopper starting with your next trip to the store. Be creative, be open-minded, and consider buying ingredients to just cook and combine in interesting ways at home. And if you find some great Paleo recipes, then by all means use them. (But don't be afraid to make some creative substitutions using this guide!)

CLOSING THOUGHTS

I hope this book has been helpful.

Are you really surprised that we feel the way we do? I know I eat like crap, my sweet-heart eats like crap (as much as I do), our little cherub eats like crap when it's up to her, and most people I know battle with this too.

The typical modern American diet has seriously been on the MUST-CHANGE path for a while!

It's interesting that this "modern" change to Paleo is basically a major flashback to a "hunter-gatherer" diet which was all the rage 10,000+ years ago.

Do you need more clues here about removing salt and processed foods from your diet, already knowing that it's clearly a dangerous part of your regular intake? I don't.

(Makes me wonder what else they knew 10,000+ years ago that we should check out!) I guess we have the best of both worlds. Their streamlined diet and my high-speed internet...

But before I wrap this up, let me tell you about our changes:

We have tried to back off on the grains, avoid sugar and corn syrup entirely, and eat fresh raw fruits and veggies all throughout the day. (Can I tell you how much I love local farmers' markets!) And we're almost always cooking now with coconut oil. I'll let you know if I lose any weight, but for now I feel inspired.

I seriously hope you enjoyed this brief ebook of lists, and that it helps you plan better shopping trips AND partake in healthier eating at restaurants. (Plus it makes a nice gift for my Mom, and all her friends)!

Good luck finding those crazy meats, BTW! And bon appetite.

DID YOU LIKE THIS?

If you enjoyed reading this book, I would love it if you would help others enjoy it as well. **LEND** it, **RECOMMEND** it, or **REVIEW** it.

You can share it with a friend via the lending feature, which has been enabled for this book. Or you can help other readers find this book by recommending it to friends and family, reading and discussion groups, online forums, or other sites. You can also review it on the site where you purchased it. If you do happen to write a review, please inform me via an email to **rachelhathawaywriter@gmail.com**, and I'll thank you with a personal email.

ABOUT THE AUTHOR: RACHEL HATHAWAY

Rachel Hathaway is the pen name for a professional writer whom you may or may not know (Mysterious, huh?). Her work spans many areas of creative fiction -- including the very wide romance genre -- as well as her published non-fiction self-help guides, personal growth and development ebooks, and a large number of articles and posts across the web on a variety of sites and blogs about smart modern shopping, style, music, the arts, and a range of eco-friendly topics. She lives in New England with her *devoted* in their dream home, and they make sure to enjoy the wonderful aspects of life on a daily basis.

ALSO BY RACHEL HATHAWAY

Beginner's Guide to Writing and Self-Publishing Romance eBooks (New Romance Writer Series) *[Also in paperback]*

Minimalism for Moms: Simplify, Declutter, and Organize Your Way to a Stress Free and Meaningful Life (Serenity at Home)

The Unofficial History of Flirting: Plus Five Ways to Reinvent Valentine's Day and Flirt Like a Bird! (Sassy Girl Series) *[Also in paperback]*

SPANISH TRANSLATIONS (Elisa Prada, translator):

Lista de alimentos para la dieta Paleo: Actualizado / Spanish Language Edition (Updated Paleo Diet Food List Book) (Serie de Nutrición) (Spanish Edition) *[Also in paperback]*

Minimalismo para Mamás: Simplifica, arregla, y organiza tu camino hacia una vida plena libre de estrés (Minimalism for Moms / Spanish edition) (Serie Serenidad en el Hogar)

LANGUAGE PREVIEW

FROM THE SPANISH TRANSLATION OF THIS BOOK: LISTA DE ALIMENTOS PARA LA DIETA PALEO (ELISA PRADA, TRANSLATOR)

FRUTAS FRESCAS Y VEGETALES

CUANDO SE TRATA de verduras en una dieta Paleo, es pan comido. Es por esto que sigue siendo totalmente posible tener nuestras noches veganas una vez a la semana.

La única cosa a tener en cuenta son las legumbres, las verduras con almidón como las papas y las frutas ricas en azúcar como el banano, que no son tan buenas para ti en cualquier plan de dieta.

Si estás atento a algunas de estas frutas y verduras en tu próxima salida de compras, puedes añadir un montón de nuevos sabores geniales a tus menús. (Me cercioré de comprar coliflor, un mango, y una bolsa de limas en una salida reciente, ¡y agregué mucha variedad a nuestra semana!) Así que aquí van:

LISTA PALEO DE FRUTAS Y VEGETALES

- Aceitunas
- Acelgas
- Aguacates
- Albaricoques
- Algas Marinas (Laminariales)
- Apio
- Arándanos
- Arándanos agrios
- Bananos (con moderación)
- Berenjena
- Berro
- Bisalto
- Brócoli
- Brotes
- Calabacín
- Calabaza
- Caqui
- Carambola
- Cebollín
- Cerezas
- Chirivía
- Ciruelas
- Col Rizada
- Col Silvestre
- Coles de Bruselas
- Coliflor

- Corazones de Alcachofa
- Cucúrbita
- Duraznos
- Endibia
- Espárragos
- Espinacas
- Frambuesas
- Fresas
- Granada
- Guayaba
- Higos
- Hojas De Mostaza
- Hongos
- Kiwi
- Lechuga Romana
- Limas
- Limones
- Litchi
- Mandarinas
- Mangos
- Manzanas
- Maracuyá
- Melón
- Moras
- Nabo Sueco
- Nabos
- Naranjas
- Papaya
- Pepino
- Peras
- Perejil
- Pimientos (Rojo, Verde, Amarillo)
- Piña
- Pomelo
- Remolacha

- Repollo
- Ruibarbo
- Sandía
- Uvas
- Zanahorias

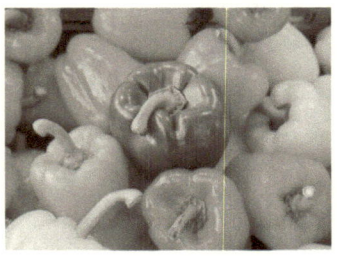

Al igual que con muchas otras dietas contemporáneas, las frutas y verduras crudas son bastante buenas para tu nivel de energía en general. También me gusta colocar un montón de estas frutas y verduras juntas en mi licuadora/máquina exprimidora y tratar de hacer una bebida GUAUSER en las mañanas, ¡pero crudas siguen siendo mejor! (Sí, usé "Guauser" como una especie de término técnico para realmente bueno. Acéptalo, no lo resistas.)

Con la cosita mezcladora justa en forma de bala en la licuadora (¡Tú sabes cual!), también podemos triturar todas las cascaras, nueces y aceites que queramos. Me siento mejor acerca de este proceso a diferencia de lo que hacíamos con nuestro viejo exprimidor, donde sentíamos que estábamos perdiendo muchas de las partes nutricionales de las frutas y verduras. (Hemos hecho recientemente algunos batidos Paleo de locos muy divertidos por ejemplo con ciruelas, fresas, un poco de espinacas, una gota de aceite de oliva y algunas semillas de calabaza... en realidad es realmente delicioso, ¡siempre y cuando utilices suficientes fresas!)

Así que, como le dije a mi mamá (¡y todo los demás en mi mundo!), eso de las frutas y verduras crudas es, POR SUPUESTO, el argumento perfecto para comprar frutas y verduras cultivadas orgánicamente. Es cierto que ellos lavan todo, que nosotros lavamos todo (¡dos veces!), pero si vas a estar comiendo cosas crudas, ¿no es mejor saber que no tuvo ningún pesticida artificial en ningún momento?

Creemos que vale totalmente la pena comprar orgánico, y puesto que todas las tiendas parecen estar uniéndose a la onda y aumentando la seguridad de los alimentos, es fácil encontrar un gran variedad de cosas.

Además, si compramos orgánico, que era la forma tradicional antes de que inventaran todos esos extraños pesticidas, entonces los precios tendrán que bajar. OK, Mamá, ya termino el sermón.

[END OF SPANISH LANGUAGE PREVIEW.]

❧

❧

THANKS FOR READING THIS BOOK!

YOUR $1500
Frugal Wedding

A SIMPLE GUIDE TO GETTING WHAT YOU WANT:
FROM TOUCHING CEREMONY TO FUN GETAWAY

RACHEL HATHAWAY

THE SMART WEDDING PLANNING GUIDE SERIES

First edition, version 1.5 • Published by RH Media.
Also available in paperback as well as in audiobook format narrated by Jackie Lauper
www.yourfrugalwedding.com
ISBN-13: 978-1547218868
ISBN-10: 154721886X

Frugal Wedding

Uncover the secrets to having the wedding you deserve for $1,500 or less.

The average wedding costs about $30,000. But it doesn't have to.

Learn creative money-saving ideas, resources, and tips to keep your beautiful, romantic, and memorable wedding from costing you a fortune.

INSTEAD OF SPENDING THOUSANDS ON ONE DAY, HAVE THE WEDDING OF YOUR DREAMS AND STILL HAVE THE RESOURCES TO:

- have a fun honeymoon getaway
- buy a house
- get out of debt
- start your married life together on secure financial footing

You want your wedding to be memorable and fun for you, your fiancee, and your guests, and you want to do it without breaking the bank.

So let's get started...

INTRODUCTION

Frugal Wedding

You're engaged?!?! [*high-pitched girlie squeal*] I am so happy for you!!! Seriously! Just thinking about you, happy reader, and the fact that you have found the love of your life, and the fact that the love of your life was smart enough to realize that you are the love of your sweetheart's life, makes me smile.

Congratulations!

Now that you two lovebirds have told your family, friends, and acquaintances, and your mother has told her family, friends, and acquaintances, and you've started using your left hand far more often just to gaze at / show off your newly acquired accessory, you've slowly and gently fluttered down from cloud nine to realize that now you actually have to...

...PLAN A WEDDING!

For most people, implementing a wedding will be the most complicated thing you ever do; not just because there are so many moving parts, but because there is an overwhelming pressure and desire to make your wedding personal and memorable. Legendary, even.

Weddings have evolved from routine events where people knew exactly what to expect, to completely customized extensions of the couple's personalities. For some, "traditional" weddings have even become unpopular, frowned upon as uncreative and bland.

Because of this, planning a wedding will probably be the first true test for the newly engaged couple. It can get very stressful balancing your tastes, your sweetie's tastes, logistical limitations, as well as the expectations of family, friends, and society, all the while trying to put your creative stamp on every aspect of the wedding.

And that's not even mentioning the budget. If you're one of those organized types who's had a binder since sixth grade of your ideal wedding, you may be in for a bit of shell shock when you start tallying up the cost of that dream wedding.

Here's the thing.

YES, your wedding IS one of the most important days of your life.

BUT... it's important because this is the day that your lives officially become connected. This is the day that you announce, publicly, in front of people who love you, that you are committed to each other through the good and the bad. This is the day that you are no longer just dating; this is the day that you are MARRIED.

And frankly, that's all anyone attending your wedding really cares about. They just want to see you and your sweetie happy. As long as you're smart about your guest list, no one at your wedding will be judging your centerpiece or menu choices. These are people who love you, and would be equally happy seeing you married in your backyard in your pajamas as on a private island resort or picturesque vineyard.

Is the dress important?

No. It's important that YOU FEEL BEAUTIFUL.

Is the venue important?

No. It's important that EVERYONE YOU LOVE IS THERE.

Are the favors important?

No. It's important that EVERYONE FEELS VALUED.

Catch my drift?

As long as you both keep things within this perspective, planning and executing a wedding can be lots of fun, and the sense of accomplishment when you see people having fun at your wedding is enough to make your heart burst.

Alright. Enough of that warm and fuzzy talk. Let's start saving.

HOW TO USE THIS BOOK

Each chapter in this book is set up with the following sections:

- **Frugal Wedding Budget Option** - This is the suggestion for the most economical way of handling that aspect of the wedding, and the best way to stay within your $1,500 budget.
- **Keep Your Cash Tips** - This is a list of ideas and suggestions if you decide on a different option than the Frugal Wedding Budget option.

Each chapter also makes the following assumptions:

- **You have to hire someone** - While I mention in multiple places throughout this book the importance of leveraging the skills, labor, and relationships of your friends and family, the Frugal Wedding Budget options given in each chapter assume you don't know anyone who can fill that role for you. After all, if your network consists of a professional cake decorator, graphic designer, wedding planner, photographer, florist, seamstress, hair stylist, restaurant owner, chef, musician, and pastor, then you shouldn't have any worries about paying for your wedding! Hopefully you'll have at least one of these covered by someone in your circle of friends and family, but these suggestions are for those of you who aren't lucky enough to be surrounded by wedding professionals.

- **You're paying** - Along those same lines, I'm assuming you and your sweetheart are paying for everything. Even though traditionally the couple's parents would provide a significant amount of financial assistance, more couples are paying for their weddings out of pocket these days. If someone in your lives offers to help pay for your Big Day, by all means, give them a hearty yes and an equally hearty hug! But remember that if someone else is paying, you can't get too picky about what they're buying. And while you shouldn't count on cash gifts as part of your wedding budget, don't forget that you are almost guaranteed to get some money from your guests, which can go a long way toward refilling that bank account.

WHERE'D YOU GET THOSE NUMBERS?

The average costs provided in this book are based on national averages pulled from various reliable sources. The actual cost may be less or more in your area. This goes for the estimated budgeted costs for each Frugal Wedding Budget option as well. The numbers provided for each Frugal Wedding Budget option aren't intended to be strict, one-size-fits-all; they're just guidelines. Depending on your priorities and tastes, your budget may look different than that offered in this book, which is as it should be.

Speaking of budget...

Frugal Wedding

*I*f you've done any research into wedding costs, you've probably run across the statistic that the average American wedding costs between $25,000-$30,000, not including the honeymoon.

THIRTY THOUSAND DOLLARS! Yikes.

Imagine someone hands you a check for $30,000. Are you REALLY going spend it on a party that lasts - on average - five hours?

If you're reading this book, you've likely already made the decision not to spend that much cash. But just in case you're still on the fence, consider this: The wedding website TheKnot in conjunction with the e-commerce site PayPal conducted a survey and found that more than one-third of couples go into debt to pay for their wedding, using credit cards or loans. Do you really want to be paying for that $1,200 wedding dress six months from now when it's just taking up space in your closet?

And even if you have the money to cash flow this expense, is spending it on a gala event the best use of that cash? Or would it be better spent as a downpayment for a house? Or a rainy day fund? Or pay down your debt?

If I still haven't convinced you, a study by two economics professors at Emory University found that couples who spend less on their wedding tend to have longer lasting marriages than those who spend more.

So there. Any way you slice it, saving money is the smarter thing to do, and there are TONS of ways to save on your wedding.

According to several sources, here's a breakdown of the national average costs for the various aspects of a wedding in the U.S.:

Wedding Planner: $1,800

Rehearsal Dinner: $1,100

Ceremony/Reception Venue: $15,100

Limousine: $730

Catering: $8,580 ($66/person x avg. guest count of 130)

Cake: $540

Invitations: $440

Dress: $1,200

Tuxedo: $250

Rings (Engagement/Wedding): $7,100

Florist/Decor: $2,000

Favors: $280

Officiant: $260

Photographer: $2,400

Videographer: $1,700

Reception Music/Band: $3,400

Ceremony Music: $600

Reception DJ: $1,000

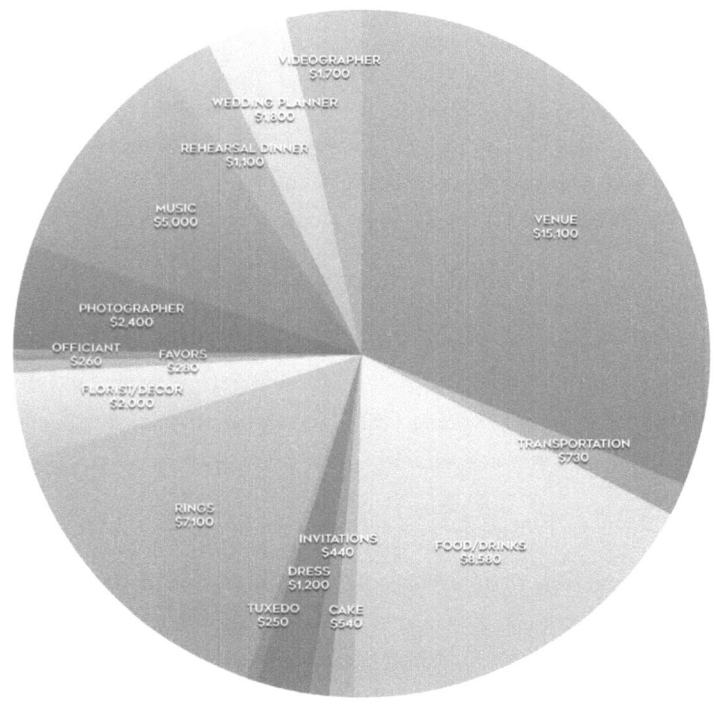

VIDEOGRAPHER
$1,700

WEDDING PLANNER
$1,800

REHEARSAL DINNER
$1,100

MUSIC
$5,000

VENUE
$15,100

PHOTOGRAPHER
$2,400

OFFICIANT
$260

FAVORS
$280

FLORIST/DECOR
$2,000

TRANSPORTATION
$730

RINGS
$7,100

INVITATIONS
$440

FOOD/DRINKS
$8,580

DRESS
$1,200

TUXEDO
$250

CAKE
$540

National Average Wedding Costs in the USA

If you were to follow this trend, your wedding would cost $48,480!!

We can do better than that!

Here are a few guiding principles that will help keep your budget low:

1. Decide what your priorities are.

When planning a wedding on a budget, you're going to have to be flexible, but if you know there are one or two non-negotiables, account for them, and figure out how you can compensate in other areas. Do you have a huge family and know that your guest list is 200 people easy? Then maybe opt for a potluck dinner instead of catering. Is it not really a wedding in your mind if it's not in a church? Unless your church will do it for free or a discounted rate, you may need to forego the formal floral arrangements.

The traditional rule of thumb is that the costs of your food (including drinks, but not cake) and venue combined should account for no more than half of your total budget, but depending on your ultimate budget and circumstance, this may not apply to you.

2. Decide what kind of wedding you want.

Do you and your sweetie prefer a formal feel, or are you laid back? Do you love a rustic aesthetic, or vintage? Deciding on an overall character and tone for your wedding will help prevent you from feeling overwhelmed, as well as steer you toward money-saving ideas.

3. Keep it Simple

For some reason, there are people who think that a wedding isn't complete without all of the expensive trappings: arches, pew ribbons, confetti, twinkle lights, boutineers, bouquets... the list goes on and on.

Obviously this is not realistic if you're planning a wedding on a budget. Take a good, hard look at everything included in a "typical" wedding, and decide whether it's truly going to add anything to your Big Day. The less stuff needed for your happy event, the less you will have to buy - and the less stuff you'll have left over to deal with after the fact.

4. Take advantage of your network.

Don't be afraid to ask for help. Believe it or not, the people around you want to help. If you know someone who is a graphic designer, ask them (nicely!) if they can design your invitations. If your sister works at a craft store, ask her to go shopping with you to get her employee discount. Does your mom have a membership at the local wholesale retailer like BJ's or Costco? Go shopping with her and see what kinds of deals you can find. Chances are you know at least one person - or someone in your network knows someone - who has a skill or situation that will help you save money. Not to mention free labor setting up/taking down chairs and tables, creating a centerpiece assembly line, and saving on delivery charges by sending your friends or family to pick up the cake, flowers, etc.

Obviously, don't take advantage of people. And it's just good manners to budget for a little extra gift for those who are doing you a favor, especially those who are giving you a service for free that they usually charge for, like musicians or photographers; spending $100 on gift cards for friends and family who helped you is a lot cheaper than paying their professional rates.

5. Stay organized.

Having an economical wedding means you will be doing a lot of the work yourself. I cannot stress enough how important keeping yourself (and your helpful team of friends and family!) organized is. The worst nightmare of any bride is to wake up the day of the wedding and realize you forgot some critical detail.

Research, planning, and execution of the myriad aspects of your wedding can get overwhelming if you don't keep track of everything. Plus, if you don't monitor your spending, you could go over budget! Eek!

Do it however you want - a simple notebook, a binder, a spreadsheet, a website, an app - whatever tool you can use to keep yourself organized. Personally, I prefer Google Drive or Evernote, but use what works best for you.

However you end up tracking, make sure you have dedicated sections for each aspect of the wedding, and make sure you write everything down, including which decisions you have to make first (venue!), who is responsible for what, budgeted cost, actual expenditures, different options, cost comparisons, delivery dates, etc.

6. Keep your guest count low.

This saves money in so many ways! You'll spend less on food, you won't need as many chairs and tables, and you can manage a smaller venue. A good rule of thumb is to only invite friends who know - or have at least met - both of you. Also consider having an adults-only wedding, which will reduce not only the guest count but the likelihood of temper tantrums ruining your romantic ceremony or magical first dance.

If you're having a hard time paring it down, consider only inviting your closest friends and immediate family, which prevents distant relatives and acquaintances from feeling slighted when they find out they weren't invited. There's also a growing trend of having the actual wedding ceremony private or family-only, and then throwing a big, casual celebration with a repetition of the vows (or not) the following summer for those who missed it the first time round.

7. Embrace used stuff.

There is an average of 2.3 million weddings per year. And you can bet a whole lot of those couples end up going home with extra centerpieces, decorations, and favors. Not to mention all of those dresses hanging in closets. Set alerts on CraigsList, eBay, Tradesy, and other reputable websites for good deals on wedding stuff. Just make sure to compare prices of used items to their actual retail cost - some people think you're going to help them recoup 100% of their investment.

Also, if the item is going to be shipped to you, try asking for pictures of the items from multiple angles to make sure it will work for you and that there are no defects. Established websites like eBay have pretty solid return policies, but you don't want to waste time on sending stuff back and starting your search all over again.

Some people feel creeped out by the thought of buying used items, especially clothing. Don't be. There are *so many* reasons buying anything used is better than buying new:

- WAY CHEAPER! - Pretty much anything used is going to be less expensive than new.
- Better Quality - Used clothing is less likely to shrink in the wash because it's already been washed. And you can rest assured that if something is used and it still looks

good, it's of a high quality and will continue to look good for you, rather than taking a gamble on brand new clothes that will start falling apart after you wear them twice.

- Supporting Your Local Community - Money spent at smaller second-hand stores is more likely to remain in your community than if you spend it at a national chain. Some thrift stores, like Savers or Salvation Army, even have relationships with local charities, so shopping there is supporting a good cause.
- Better for the Environment - Buying used supports the used goods industry, which reduces the amount of landfill waste. Decreasing demand for new items means less consumption of resources and reduced global shipping emissions. Bonus!
- Did I mention that used stuff is WAY CHEAPER!!

If you're still not convinced, remember that people often donate brand new clothing and items with the tag still on it to second-hand stores. These items will still be severely marked down from the retail cost, so you can support the cycle of reuse and save money without having any case of the creeps.

8. Think local and in-season.

Do a little research to find out which foods and flowers are ripe and blooming naturally in your area at the time of your wedding. If you're getting married in winter, then a strawberry-filled cake and a bouquet of daisies aren't the most budget-conscious choices.

Along those lines, because of increased demand, flowers cost more (as in 15% to 30% more) near Easter, Mother's Day, Valentine's Day, and prom season, so try to keep your wedding far, far away from these holidays.

9. Shop the sales, and don't the forget coupons!

Take a close look at those junk mail flyers before you recycle them, as they often include notices of sales in your neighborhood. Every time there's a holiday, there is a clearance sale immediately after:

- Valentine's Day - great for decorations such as vases and ribbon
- Easter - look for baskets, pretty stationery, flower girl dresses, and shoes for everyone in the wedding party
- Fourth of July - perfect stuff for your outdoor wedding: tiki torches, flatware, and outdoor tablecloths
- Halloween - black vases, pumpkins
- Thanksgiving - beautiful decorations for your fall wedding
- Christmas - think lights, greenery, and tablecloths

Before you go to any store, be sure to check their website for coupons. Craft stores, big box stores, you name it - they almost all have coupons on their website, or will send you one if you sign up for their newsletter.

Many stores now have their own coupon apps, with coupons that may not be available on their website. If a coupon is only good for a limited number of items per visit, bring a friend (or two, or five!) and make separate purchases to get the most out of your shopping trips so you don't have to waste gas going to the store over and over.

10. Save big with rebate and discount websites.

Websites such as FatWallet (see our resource chapter at the end) give you rebates on purchases made through their site. Amazon also has Amazon Warehouse, which sells open-box items or items with damaged packaging at discounted rates. Get discounted gift cards at Raise for the stores you're going to shop at, and set alerts so you'll know as soon as a new card is available.

11. Venture outside of your usual shopping places.

Drive around your neighborhood and look at all of the stores you don't usually go to. Stop in and see what they have to offer - especially if you see the word "SALE" in their window!

If you're like me, you frequent the big box stores where you can get everything in one trip. While you may not usually shop at dollar stores or discount stores, these places may have what you're looking for at lower prices. Don't drive around too much though - you don't want to spend all your savings on gas.

Look online as well at your regular retail stores and those other stores; you may find even better selection, but don't let shipping costs eat into your savings.

12. Use your credit card points.

If you have a credit card with cash back points and 0% APR, then go ahead and charge as much as you can. Just DON'T FORGET to pay it back BEFORE the interest charges kick in though.

13. Give yourself plenty of time.

There's no getting around it: Planning a wedding on a budget just takes longer than spending haphazardly. You want to be able to take advantage of seasonal and clearance sales at stores, compare prices, as well as leave yourself (and Team Wedding) time to make any DIY wedding projects. Spreading out the expenses over a year also feels a lot less painful than spending it all in three months.

14. Saving money doesn't have to mean skimping on style.

Just because your wedding isn't going to cost a gazillion dollars doesn't mean it can't look like it did. This goes hand in hand with the "give yourself time" concept, because getting things to look beautiful and stylish will take a lot of creativity and experimentation.

15. Be realistic.

You can't do everything. Being realistic about your time, abilities, and preferences will help keep planning and executing your wedding an enjoyable experience. If you don't like doing crafts, then don't try to make your own invitations. If you've never really baked before, don't try to make your cake.

If you do want to do everything, and you do actually have the appropriate skill sets, be realistic about your timeline. Floral arrangements, making the cake, and decorating the venue are just a few of the activities that need to happen the day before or day of the wedding. You can't wear yourself ragged and be too exhausted to enjoy your own wedding. Don't be afraid to delegate to friends or family, or spend a little money early in the process to reduce last minute stress.

16. Think about after the wedding.

Even if you don't spend much, it's a bummer to buy something you're only going to use once. Buying items you know you can use again will give you that much more bang for your buck.

If you can't use something again, sell it! Continue the cycle of Happy Couples helping Happy Couples.

17. Remember, this is YOUR wedding.

While it's wonderful that people want to help, sometimes they feel that they need to offer their opinions as well. You don't have to hold the ceremony at a certain venue simply because your parents were married there, and you don't have to buy the dress that your sister insists is perfect for you even though it's way too expensive. You and your lovey are the only ones who truly matter here. Thank others for their advice and move on.

Now that we've covered the big picture stuff, let's talk details...

VENUE & TRANSPORTATION

Frugal Wedding

Wedding Venue

National Average Cost: $15,100

The venue is the first wedding decision you need to make. If you've started looking around for places to have your wedding, you know that there are lots of options. Many cities and towns offer a variety of event centers, halls, and churches, but they'll charge you for tablecloths and chair upgrades, add on cleaning fees, and request even more money if you want to serve alcohol. A lot of venues will even require you to use their approved vendors, such as DJs, caterers, and bartenders, immediately upping the cost.

So what do you do...?

Outdoor Wedding
Your Frugal Wedding Budget: $0 - $300

Outdoor venues, such as a local park or farm, require little or no decoration and usually don't cost a thing. A gazebo in someone's well-landscaped backyard, or even a garden nursery center (which is also usually tented - bonus!), can be a perfect setting for your wedding.

Consider scouting ceremony sites at a local lake or beach if you live near one; it's simple and classic. Just make sure it's very clear in the invitations that the wedding in on a beach, so people come prepared with appropriate footwear (or lack thereof).

State and national parks can provide a beautiful background, and many of them have pavilions you can use for your reception. Some also have playgrounds, so any children of your guests will have instant entertainment. Ask about parking fees and recreation permit fees, which can run pretty high. There is a caveat here: Be sure to check out the restroom facilities - not all park bathrooms are created equal.

Of course, an outdoor wedding is always subject to mother nature, and you'll need to factor in the cost of reserving - and potentially using - a large tent, which can take a big chunk out of your budget.

Check out other local attractions that could provide a unique venue for your wedding, such as a zoo, botanical garden, historical site, or museum. Some of these may charge a small fee or donation, and others may not. You'll have to call and check around, because each one will be different.

If you belong to a church, you may be able to use the building for free, or pay a small fee to use an adjacent hall or room for your reception.

Whichever venue you decide on, make sure you book it early. You must have the date confirmed before you make any other plans. Some venues may book up fast depending on the time of year (September and October are currently the most popular months for marriages), and you may not get the date you desire if you don't act quickly.

KEEP YOUR CASH TIPS

If the frugal outdoor wedding isn't for you, here are some other ways you can save money on your venue:

All-in-One - Having your ceremony and your reception at the same venue not only saves money but time and stress as well. Simply ask your ushers to move back a few of the tables to make a dance floor. Your guests won't have to travel to a reception (this is especially good for out-of-town or elderly guests), and you won't have to pay twice.

Choose your date wisely - Saturday is the most expensive day to have a wedding. Ask your desired venue about their Sunday or weekday rates. Yes, weekday weddings are unexpected, but everyone will have plenty of notice to take the day off. Unless they're willing to help pay for the venue fee, don't let anyone's mutterings of discontent bother you! A weekday wedding can also be less expensive for people who have to travel, as rates are generally lower during the week.

Getting married in the off-season will also save you on venue costs. June through September are peak wedding months and therefore the most expensive, with winter months being the cheapest. Just like weddings have an off-season, wedding professionals do too, so you'll save on photographers, musicians, and others.

Rent a house - Finding a beautiful house for the weekend in a lovely area is super easy on sites like AirBNB. Not only will it serve as the perfect wedding venue, it can be reception hall and honeymoon suite as well. Being upfront that you'll be using their house in this way, and maintaining good communication with the homeowner will ensure a positive experience on both sides.

Colleges and Universities - If you live near a historic college campus, chances are the dining hall is gorgeous with wood beams, high ceilings, and a gigantic fireplace. Or maybe they have a chapel on campus you can reserve on the cheap. If you know an employee, alumni, or current student, have them make the call to see if they'll get a discount.

Tables & Chairs

National Average Cost: $354-1,670

Even if you've found the right venue, your guests need a place to sit, eat, and visit with each other. You can contact a rental company for this, but their prices might be a little more than you're willing to pay. They may also charge you a fee if the tables and chairs aren't immaculate when you return them.

Borrow/Rent from Church or Lodge
Your Frugal Wedding Budget: $50

Local lodges, like the Elks, VFW, or American Legion, always have a lot of tables on hand. Contact the ones in your area to see if they would be willing to rent them to you and how much they would charge. You will probably need to have a way to pick them up and return them, so make sure you have a friend with a truck if you can't do it yourself. Churches are also prepared for large gatherings, and may be willing help you out either for free or a small fee. Again, you'll probably need to transport them yourself.

KEEP YOUR CASH TIPS

The Bigger the Better - The bigger your tables are, the fewer centerpieces and tablecloths you'll need.

Tablecloths - If your tables are free or inexpensive, you may need to spend some money on tablecloths, as they may not match or be in perfect condition. Tablecloths will hide these inconsistencies and stains, and your guests will never know the difference.

Check out post-holiday clearance sales for table coverings, and be sure to look at party stores and dollar stores as well. If you're having difficulty finding tablecloths that aren't too expensive, you could always make your own. Go to craft stores and find fabric on sale that matches your wedding colors. Some stores even have clearance fabrics for as low as a dollar per yard, which makes a pretty cheap tablecloth. Just hem up the edges (or have a friend do it).

Rule of Thumb - When you're counting up the chairs and tables you'll need, overestimate by 10%. This will accommodate any guests that didn't RSVP but decided to show up anyway. It also leaves enough space for anyone you have hired (such as a photographer, DJ, or officiant) to sit down and eat.

Transportation

National Average Cost: $730

Drive Yourself
Your Frugal Wedding Budget: $0

Do you really need a stretch limo SUV or horse-drawn carriage? Think about your entrance and exit. Is anyone even going to see you?

My husband and I thought that it wouldn't be romantic driving ourselves from the ceremony to the reception, but we just couldn't validate spending hundreds of dollars on something we were fully capable of doing ourselves. And it actually turned out to be the perfect choice. We were the last ones to leave the ceremony venue and arrive at the reception venue, so no one saw our "unromantic" exit or entrance, and it was nice being alone, quietly holding hands, without feeling like someone was watching us or listening to us talk.

If you really don't want to drive yourselves, ask a friend or family member to play chauffeur. It can be nice to have a quiet moment with someone (else) you love in the middle of the hustle and bustle of your Big Day.

FOOD & DRINKS

Frugal Wedding

Food & Drinks

National Average Cost: $8,580

Feeding your guests can be a huge expense, especially if you have it catered. Catering companies typically charge per guest, and the average couple will spend $66 per plate. Some caterers don't even include dishes, flatware, and serving your guests in their base charge.

Potluck Wedding
Your Frugal Wedding Budget: $300

While they may not be as popular now, potluck weddings have historically been the norm. People just didn't have the resources to feed everyone, so the whole community contributed. Nowadays, potluck weddings are a great alternative to expensive catering, as long as it's handled properly:

- **Don't run out of the main dish** - Even at potluck weddings, the couple often provides the main dish to make sure there is enough for everyone. If you're not going to take on that expense, make sure you get a few different people to bring the same thing to constitute the main entree, so no one's left hungry.

- **Keep it optional** - Not everyone is going to want to bring a dish, and some just won't be able to - you can't expect people who are traveling to cook. You don't want anyone feeling stressed about this, so include "Yes/No" check boxes on your invitation for bringing a dish.

- **Say goodbye to the registry** - If you're having a potluck wedding, etiquette demands that you drop the registry. People are saving you thousands of dollars by bringing food, so just accept that as your gift and buy your own toaster.

- **Keep it organized** - The biggest issue with potluck weddings is keeping the meal balanced. One way to do that is assign types of dishes by guests' first initials: A-D bring appetizers, E-H bring salads, I-L brings bread or dinner rolls, etc. Remember that redundancy is a good thing - you want multiple people bringing the same dish to ensure that everyone gets a balanced meal. Either you or someone on Team Wedding will need to keep track of the menu, monitoring the invitations and determining whether someone needs to switch dish types to avoid a pasta salad glut. Someone (not you or your sweetheart!) will also need to coordinate the day of, letting people know where to put their meals, making sure sternos are lit, confirming plates and flatware are abundant, and everything else that will make the meal run smoothly.

- **It's not free** - Even a potluck won't be completely free. Unless you're having your reception at a church or somewhere that already has supplies, you'll need to invest in serving utensils, plates, flatware, napkins, buffet pans, and sterno cans.

And remember that even if you do have access to the venue's dishes, you could very well spend your first day of marriage of washing dishes, which may not cost anything, but isn't particularly romantic.

KEEP YOUR CASH TIPS

Afternoon Tea - Instead of a full meal, do an "afternoon tea" reception, offering snacks, hors d'oeuvres, and other finger foods. You can prepare these simple foods the day before and refrigerate. It will be easy to accommodate the tastes of all your guests regardless of religious preferences or allergies. Children especially love these kinds of meals. You can also do a dessert-only reception, with a vast array of yummy sweets. This idea is great for rehearsal dinner as well (although you may not get away with doing it for both...)!

Build Your Own Meal Bars - Let your guests make their own meal with a taco bar, waffle bar, or even a baked potato bar. This is a great way to display the food, and your guests will be happy because they can have their meal just the way they like it. Another benefit is that you don't need anyone to serve, because the guests serve themselves.

Food Truck - If you live near a city, chances are there are lots of amazing food trucks in your vicinity, and most would be thrilled to be hired for a private event. A food truck is perfect for catering outdoor receptions, and offer a wide variety of cuisine from tacos to crepes. They're also much cheaper than an actual caterer, and can offer a level of customization for your guests, although you'll want to limit the menu to just one or two options to keep your costs down. Check out food truck locator websites like RoamingHunger, or just take a walk around your city and sample different trucks. Obviously compare food quality, but also take note of kitchen cleanliness and servers' attitudes.

Backyard Barbecue - A grill and some coolers make a great party, no matter what the occasion. Grab a guy or gal who loves to grill and put them in charge of the hot dogs, hamburgers, or brats. Or go a bit more upscale and do a lobster boil or clambake on the beach. Ask your guests to bring sides such as fresh corn on the cob, homemade cole slaw, or fruit. Barbecues are perfect for the couple with laid back style, and they pair nicely with outdoor weddings.

DIY - Yes, you can even choose to feed your guests yourself! You'll spend money on the ingredients, but not nearly as much as if you used a caterer. Choose foods that can be made ahead and frozen to save yourself stress the day before the wedding. Good options include lasagna, soups, meatballs, spaghetti sauce, and meatloaf. Simply defrost and you're good to go. Stock up on ingredients ahead of time to spread the cost out over several months and take advantage of any sales. Make sure you have someone in charge of laying out the food so you don't have to worry about it on the Big Day.

Restaurant - Having your reception at a restaurant means you don't have to pay for servers, flatware, tables, or chairs. Find one that either has a nice decor already, or one that will allow you to bring in your own centerpieces, to ensure you get the ambience you're looking for.

Drinks/Alcohol - Alcohol is just plain expensive, and some venues charge you an extra fee if you plan to serve it at your wedding. You can save quite a bit of money skipping it entirely and let people toast with whatever they're drinking. If it's important to you, have a cash bar and let your guests know ahead of time. You could also provide a keg or a couple boxes of wine. Lots of couples are also opting to have a single "signature" drink, instead of an array of different alcohol. Buy drinks in bulk at a warehouse store such as BJ's or Sam's Club. (Coolers full of sodas and bottled water means that you don't need to buy cups.)

Plates and Flatware - A warehouse store comes in handy once again when it comes to setting the table. Many bulk stores have a selection of plates and flatware that are on the nicer side, and they will cost much less than what a caterer would charge. Plus, you get to keep any extras and use them at home!

Dessert

National Average Cost: $540+

When you think of a wedding cake, you probably imagine a frosted monstrosity of at least three tiers. The average wedding cake costs $540, and some couples even buy extra cakes to make sure there is enough for all of the guests. If you're doing a wedding on a budget, this just isn't an option.

Let Them Eat Sheet Cake...
Your Frugal Wedding Budget: $130

Cake is cake, am I right? Just buy a couple of sheet cakes from the grocery store - they might even pre-slice them for you if you ask nicely. Economical couples have been pulling the sheet cake switcheroo (getting a fancy cake for cutting, and then serving their guests sheet cake) for years anyway. Why not just pull back the curtain and reveal the truth: that you're too smart to spend $500 on a cake!

KEEP YOUR CASH TIPS

Shop Local - Check out small, locally owned bakeries to see if you can get a better deal. You might also find someone on CraigsList who bakes out of their home and will charge you far less than a larger cake shop. When ordering your cake, go for buttercream or cream cheese frosting instead of fondant; it's less expensive and tastes better!

Call a Friend - Have a friend or family member that enjoys time in the kitchen? Try to score a cake for free or for the cost of supplies and ingredients. It doesn't have to be a huge, elaborate cake to be memorable, and cake decorating has become a popular hobby.

Potluck It - If you're having a potluck dinner, why not the dessert too! You can either have a bunch of people bring the same thing, or just treat it like the rest of the potluck and let people choose their own dish.

Other Sweet Ideas - While cakes are traditional, other desserts are now trendy wedding alternatives. You could have wedding doughnuts, cookies, cheesecakes, or cupcakes. Five trays of pastries at your local bakery costs about the same as two sheet cakes, gives people more options, and eliminates the need for extra forks and plates.

INVITATIONS

Frugal Wedding

Invitations

National Average Cost: $440+

Invitations are the first impressions your guests will get of your wedding. Your guests will not only learn the date and time of your wedding, but how they should dress and whether or not they should come hungry. In short, they're a lot more than just a piece of paper.

Make Them Yourself
Your Frugal Wedding Budget: $75

Many word processing programs come with built-in templates for invitations that you can easily customize. Do a couple of test prints to make sure they look good before you print all of them. Pick up a few packages of blank cards that come with their own envelopes. If your printer can't handle the thicker paper, print it at an office supply store.

Don't forget to triple-proofread (you, your fiancee, and a friend) your invitations before printing - you don't want to have to pay twice for your supplies because of a single lousy typo!

You can also make your invitations with rubber stamps and other card making supplies from your local craft store. Get your friends or your fiancee to help you and make a fun evening of it. Buy a chisel-tip marker and practice your "calligraphy" skills before addressing all of those envelopes, or just print out labels using a pretty font on your computer.

Either way you do it, keep your invitations easy to read, and ensure that they contain all of the information your guests will need. Stick with standard envelope sizes and keep the embellishments (ribbon, gems) to a minimum to avoid extra postage fees. Postage for postcards is even cheaper than sending invitations in envelopes, and are a particularly good idea if guests can RSVP electronically.

KEEP YOUR CASH TIPS

Skip Save the Dates - As soon as you have a hard date, contact the people you think may need an extra heads up by phone or email. As long as you get your invitations out to everyone else at least two or three months before your wedding, they should have enough time to make the necessary arrangements.

Go Electronic - In this day and age, there are lots of ways to reach your guests without using paper or postage. You can simply send out emails, but you need to make sure you send follow up reminders. There are also lots of websites that enable you to create a website specifically for your wedding, such as TheKnot, all for free. You can manage RSVPs, the menu, your registry, and any wedding-related information all in one central location. If emails seem too informal, make a fun video to send to everyone with the relevant details.

Remember that you probably have some guests, such as older relatives, who aren't comfortable responding electronically. You'll still need to get all of the information to them somehow, either with a phone call or a paper invitation.

RSVP - Even if you do send paper invitations, you can still cut down on your paper and postage costs by asking your guests to RSVP electronically. Set up a new email account or simply ask them to text or call. There are several RSVP websites available, but be careful to find one that's actually free.

Frugal Wedding

*W*hat the *Happy Couple* wears on the Big Day can take up a huge chunk of your overall budget. Most couples spend as much as 15% of their budget on the dress, tux, and rings.

It's also probably the most important of your expenses, because - there's no getting around it - everyone is going to be staring at you all day. Add onto that decades of looking at those pictures, and you definitely want to look your best. However, you're also going to be wearing these clothes for several hours (unless you change after the ceremony), so you need to be comfortable.

Let's break this down and see where we can start saving...

The Dress

National Average Cost: $1,200

It's easy to say that you're not going to spend more than "X" amount of dollars on your dress. But take a lesson from me: I made the mistake of settling for a less expensive dress that didn't fit quite right. Despite several sessions with the tailor (which, thank goodness, were included with the dress purchase - always ask about that!), I still didn't feel all that comfortable in the dress on the day of my wedding. So don't be afraid to spend a little more than you anticipated if it's going to make the difference between gazing fondly at your pictures after the fact, or spending your time cropping out unflattering armpit fat you didn't realize you had. Just make sure to accommodate for this change elsewhere in your overall budget.

Buy Used or Rent
Your Frugal Wedding Budget: $150

Buy Used - When buying a used dress, have a friend take your measurements so you know exactly what you need, as wedding dress sizes are often not the same as your regular clothing size. Also ask the seller about any alterations that have already been done, so you know exactly what you're getting.

The Bad News...

You are most likely not going to find your dream dress at a thrift store or yard sale, or on eBay or Craigslist. What you will find are tons and tons of inexpensive dresses that are beautiful but not your size, or have too many ruffles, or not enough lace.

The Good News...

Dresses can be tailored! Buying a $50 dress that is five sizes too big and having it sized down can still be less expensive than a new dress. However, be sure to call around to local tailors with your list of expected alterations BEFORE you buy the dress to get an idea of how much it will cost. Sizing it down may only be $50, but adding or removing materials can cost a few hundred dollars, which defeats the purpose of buying a used dress.

And of course, don't forget that taking a dress in is usually an easy task, but letting one out may be impossible, so steer clear of dresses that are too small for you, even if you're on a wedding diet!

Rent - Why buy a dress at all? Websites such as Borrowing Magnolia, Nearly Newlywed, and Rent the Runway have all had good press about the high quality of their rentable dresses. Call up their customer service to find out exactly how it works to make sure you don't get zinged with any penalty fees for keeping a dress too long.

KEEP YOUR CASH TIPS

Borrow - You may not have to spend a dime if someone has a dress they're willing to loan or give you. After asking your mom, check around and see if an older cousin or aunt has a dress you can use. You're more likely to have luck with older relatives who are further away from their wedding day, as people closer to your age are probably still emotionally attached to and possessive of their gowns. Just make sure you double-check with your dress angel if you need to make alterations!

Clearance/Sample Sales - Bridal store sales are both good and bad. Obviously they're good because you're theoretically getting a better price on an expensive dress. They're bad because you really don't have the time to sit around and wait for a sale to buy your dress. Also, the selection will be limited, and items on clearance most likely do not come with any alterations, so you could still end up spending serious money on a tailor. You may also need to pay for dress cleaning out of pocket, which can be very expensive due to the fine fabrics and multiple layers.

Most wedding dress sales happen in late winter or early spring, when these retailers have to make room for the new dresses they've ordered for the coming season. If you're already past this point in the year, don't count on a sale as your saving grace. Go ahead and sign up for the email newsletters of all of the bridal boutiques in your area just in case, but don't stop looking elsewhere.

Etsy - While most likely more expensive than buying a used dress, a handmade dress by someone on Etsy will still be less expensive than bridal stores, especially if you have a simple design. A friend of mine had a kimono-style dress made on Etsy for $400, which isn't cheap, but she didn't need any alterations. Just be sure to triple-check your measurements, because most sellers won't do refunds for custom-made dresses.

Go Non-Traditional - When I was shopping for dresses, I had what I thought was the brilliant idea of going to department stores and just finding a nice white formal dress that wasn't labeled a "wedding dress." Well, I had no luck. I looked online. Still no luck.

I'm betting there's a secret understanding between these stores and the wedding industry to never have white formal wear, to avoid people such as myself circumventing the inflated cost of anything associated with weddings.

Arrgh!! Why is everything for weddings SO EXPENSIVE?!?!?!?

Anyway... My idea of a "non-traditional" wedding dress was actually pretty traditional, because I was still looking for white formal wear. Consider other colors, other styles. My sister got married in a white tank top and white skirt, and changed into shorts afterward to play volleyball with her guests, and still looked gorgeous.

Just remember that if you opt for a color other than white, you're not going to stand out as much, because no one wears white to a wedding, but they could wear green, pink, or red. To avoid blending in with the crowd too much, consider asking everyone else to wear white (or black and white) so you're the only one wearing color.

The Tux

National Average Cost: $250

Pretty much all of the strategies above apply to the tuxedo as well.

Luckily, renting a tux is the standard for the groom, so it's not as much of a hassle as it is for the bride. However, consider going the non-traditional route to save even more.

Suit Up... or Not
Your Frugal Wedding Budget: $0

Does the groom already have a nice suit that fits well? If not, consider buying one. It may cost the same as a rental, but a suit is one of those things that comes in handy for future formal events, thus reducing your future expenses. He can always spice up his existing suit with a new vest, fancy cufflinks, or a French cuff shirt.

If you're having a laid back or casual style wedding, let the groom join in the fun by wearing a nice button-down shirt and dress pants, which he should also already own.

The Rings

National Average Cost: $7,100+

Ah, the rings: symbols of your commitment to each other, of your eternal bond.

But that's all they are: a symbol. Any *specialness* attached to your wedding rings exists only because *you make them special*. Therefore, any ring from anywhere will do the trick, as long as it's of good quality and will last as long as your marriage.

Buy Used
Your Frugal Wedding Budget: $50

Engagement rings and wedding bands at retail jewelry stores can cost thousands of dollars. This is a perfect time to look for used bling on

Tradesy, eBay, CraigsList, or even at local pawn shops. Even most online wedding ring retailers will have pre-owned sections with rings going for half the cost.

Unfortunately, rings at antique stores are usually pricey because they've gone from being "used" to that nebulous, somehow more valuable, label of "antique." And don't worry about that silly superstition that rings from an unsuccessful marriage are bad luck. It's not uncommon for women to sell their rings simply because they got new ones. Besides, you and your lovey are soulmates.

Remember, just because you're on a budget now, doesn't mean you'll always be on one. Someday you and your sweetheart will be feeling more prosperous, and you can "surprise" each other with a new set as an anniversary gift (after you've both had fun shopping for your favorites...).

If you're really hoping for fancy-looking new rings, you can find knockoff designer wedding rings on eBay, and unique or non-traditional rings on Etsy or Amazon. If you do buy a ring online, make sure you triple-check your ring size at a local jeweler. Some rings can be sized within reason, but it doesn't always turn out well depending on how the ring was made. Also check if there are any reviews for the ring, and learn from others who have been burned by cheap workmanship.

Shoes & Other Accessories

National Average Cost: $250+

Don't forget to budget for shoes, jewelry, veils, crowns, or whatever else the bride wants as part of her attire. "Bridal" shoes can retail for $200+, which is pretty ridiculous. Remember our guiding principle of thinking about what you can use after the wedding, and try to find fancy shoes that you will wear with other outfits.

Or...

Raid Your Closet
Your Frugal Wedding Budget: $0

Keep it simple, using accessories you already own or can borrow (something borrowed: check!), and your bank account will thank you.

Frugal Wedding

Hair and Makeup

National Average Cost: $200+

There's no doubt you want to feel magical on your wedding day, and your hair and makeup are just as much a part of that as your dress. If you decide to have a professional help you, it's likely to cost over $200 between both a trial run appointment and the actual wedding day appointment. Whether or not this expense is worth it depends on what you envision yourself looking like on the Big Day, and whether you have a stylist you can trust to do what you want. If you're terrible at hair and makeup, then it might be a good thing to budget for.

Do It Yourself
Your Frugal Wedding Budget: $0

You know how you like your makeup to look. While many brides think they need something completely different to be glamorous, this isn't necessarily true. A little extra eye makeup and a new shade of lipstick can be just enough to edge you into princess status. You want to wear enough makeup to look good for pictures, but not so much that it's embarrassing for your guests to see you in real life.

The same goes for your hair. You've been styling your hair for most of your life, so you're familiar with its texture and natural part. You also know what it will and won't do. This gives you more of an advantage than you realize. Try different styles and wear them around for the day to see how they hold up. A hair style that falls down after an hour is only going to cause you frustration. Make sure you pick a look that fits well with your current cut and the texture of your hair for best results.

For both your hair and your makeup, check out the numerous tutorials available on YouTube. Make sure you practice your style choice several times well before the Big Day.

Ask a Friend - Once again, your friends and family can come to the rescue here! Do you have an aunt that runs a beauty salon? Or a friend that had gone to school for cosmetology before she decided to be a nurse instead? Pull on the talents of those around you, and you can probably find someone who can do it for free. You still need to make sure that you have a couple of practice sessions to ensure you achieve your desired look and that it will hold up.

BRIDESMAIDS & GROOMSMEN

Frugal Wedding

*A*lthough not technically part of your wedding budget, since the wedding party usually pays for their own dresses and tuxes, you can still help them save money too. After all, you're probably not the only one on a budget. Plus, if you keep them from having to pay hundreds of dollars on clothes, you may get an even better wedding present...

Let your bridesmaids' personalities shine too - With low-budget and highly personalized weddings as the norm these days, identical dresses for the bridesmaids is less expected. Pull from your wedding color scheme and just ask all the bridesmaids to stick to the same color and style (e.g. calf-length lavender dress). This allows your bridesmaids to select dresses that work with their body types, instead of forcing a one-size-fits-all ideal.

Note that this strategy will only work as long as your colors are simple. Black and white? They've got it covered. Dark magenta and cyan? Maybe not so much. If you have a very specific and off-shade color scheme, consider giving them swatches to shop with.

Department Stores - Bridal stores aren't the only places with pretty dresses. Browse through the formal section of your local department store. This is an especially good resource for junior bridesmaids and flower girls when holiday dresses go on clearance. Even the full price is likely to be less than half of what you would find at a bridal retailer.

Go Casual - Be open to outfits that aren't as formal. This can provide a fun atmosphere to your wedding, and they will definitely be less expensive than formalwear. Bridesmaids can wear skirts or sundresses, and groomsmen can wear suits, button-down shirts, or even t-shirts. As long as it fits with your colors and the vibe of your Big Day, go for it.

CENTERPIECES, FAVORS, & DECOR

Frugal Wedding

Decor

National Average Cost: $2,000

---

*M*ost venues will need a little sprucing up. Centerpieces and other decorations not only look nice, but also bring the whole room together with your wedding theme. But when you add up the cost of centerpieces from a florist, decorations for the food tables, and any other trimmings such as pew bows, it can get pretty pricey.

Do It Yourself
Your Frugal Wedding Budget: $50

This is one place where your (or a friend's) DIY skills will really come in handy. This is the perfect time to have your friends and family over for a centerpiece-making party. Choose centerpieces that don't require fresh flowers so you can make them ahead of time. Making centerpieces that can double as guest favors is a great money-saving strategy as well.

Not sure what to do? Here are just a few ideas that use low- or no-cost materials:

- mason jars or vases with floating tea lights or candles in sand
- inflated balloons wrapped in tulle and tied down with ribbon
- potted plants (grow them yourself and they're even cheaper!)
- cut up thick tree branches into discs and put a single, large flower head in the middle
- bowls of fruit
- gourds
- paper lanterns
- stacks of books
- framed artistic photographs of places or things you both love
- succulents
- create your own wedding "logo" (monogram or graphic icon) and stencil, stamp, and print it onto everything wedding-related; this can make items that may not look the same still feel cohesive

KEEP YOUR CASH TIPS

Ceremony Decorations - An arch is nice, but not necessary. If you do decide that this is a must-have, check Craigslist or Facebook swap groups to see if you can find one used. Or take a peek at Pinterest for other backdrop ideas.

Hit the Lights - Christmas lights are a great addition to food tables, arches, and other decorations. You probably have plenty hiding in your basement. The ones with white wires (as opposed to green) typically work the best for tables and arches, but the green ones are fine if you're weaving them into greenery or decorative trees.

Outdoor Wedding = Less Decorations - Having your wedding in a setting that is already full of flowers and naturally beautiful scenery, like a park, garden nursery, or botanical center, will significantly reduce your decorating budget. Even if the venue is a bit more expensive, compare it to the cost of decorations and see which is actually cheaper.

Favors

National Average Cost: $280+

While you could try to get away without giving favors, this is one of the best ways to let your personality as a couple shine, and there are plenty of ways to do so creatively and inexpensively.

Escort Card Favors
Your Frugal Wedding Budget: $50

A great way to save money is for your escort cards to double as favors. You can also give one favor per couple for added savings. Here are a few ideas:

- **Mix CDs** - Fill these with your (and your sweetie's) favorite tunes. Use paper CD envelopes and find someone with nice handwriting and a chiseled marker to write the names and seating arrangements on the back.
- **Wine Glasses** - Frequent thrift stores for wine glasses on the cheap, and tie the place cards to stems with ribbon. This will only really work if you have wine at your wedding though... And don't forget to wash them!
- **Candy Buffet** - Make a table of candies in your wedding colors, and give each guest a personalized baggie. Let them create their own perfect and sweet favor.
- **Keep it Useful** - Whatever you decide to use for favors, it will still be a waste of your money and/or time if people don't

take them home. Edible or practical gifts are the best route, rather than fancy and frivolous.

- **Centerpieces** - I know I said it already, but just in case you missed it: centerpieces can double as favors as well!

Guest Book

National Average Cost: $60

While the guest book is not the most notable expense on any wedding list, it's definitely an expense worth scrutinizing. Any pretty blank book you like will do - just make sure it will lay flat easily.

Or how about you...

Get Creative
Your Frugal Wedding Budget: $20

There are lots of new, non-traditional, and low-cost ideas for guest "books":

- puzzle pieces
- poster
- large photo matte that you can use later for your wedding photo
- find a used photography book filled with pictures that go with the theme of your wedding - people can sign the inside covers, or on the pages themselves
- buy the album you're going to use for your wedding pictures or scrapbook before the Big Day, and have your guests get it started for you by signing all over
- baseball caps
- Jenga pieces

- a pretty piece of fabric or quilt

Card Box or Wishing Well
Your Frugal Wedding Budget: $5

A cardboard box covered in pretty paper costs next to nothing!

If you do decide to purchase a box or bird cage, make sure it's one that you'd like to see on your mantle when the wedding is over.

Frugal Wedding

Flowers

National Average Cost: $2,000+

---

lowers can help give your venue a more romantic atmosphere. They'll also be featured in almost all of your photographs, so it's important to find ones that fit your style and taste. In addition to a bridal bouquet, you may also want bridesmaids' bouquets; boutonnieres for the groom, groomsmen, ring bearer, and fathers; corsages for the mothers; and petals for the flower girl. Don't forget the toss bouquet! It really adds up, but the great thing is that there are lots of ways to get beautiful flowers on a budget.

Grow and Arrange Them Yourself
Your Frugal Wedding Budget: $20

A true do-it-yourself idea is to check out what flowers are in bloom around your wedding date and grow them yourself! All you have to buy are the seeds or bulbs. This works even better if you or a family member already has a garden with well-established flowering plants, such as hydrangeas, lilacs, or tulips.

A close alternative to growing them is buying them at the Farmer's Market, depending on what time of year you're getting married. They are usually far cheaper than you would find at any stores, and they're from local farms.

If arranging fresh flowers yourself, make sure you leave yourself plenty of time the night before your wedding to do it. If you think you'll be too busy the night before, ask a friend.

KEEP YOUR CASH TIPS

Less is More - Instead of giving each of your bridesmaids an entire bouquet, give them just one flower - just make sure it's big and bright enough to stand out.

Double Duty - If you do get bouquets for you and the bridesmaids, consider using them again as centerpieces. Assign someone the task of collecting all of them after the ceremony and dropping them into the empty vases before everyone else shows up at the reception.

Skip the Florist - Grocery stores have the same flowers as florist boutiques for a fraction of the price. Some might even make the bouquets for you.

Use Artificial Flowers - Silk or other fabric flowers are a great alternative for those who want to keep things easy and inexpensive. You can arrange them months in advance, with plenty of time to decide what looks good. You'll never have to worry about keeping them fresh, and the wedding party can keep their bouquets and boutonnieres as keepsakes. Watch the sales flyers at your local craft stores to get artificial flowers for a discounted price.

Don't Use Them - While many people expect flowers at a wedding, it doesn't mean you have to use them. You can make lots of great centerpieces that don't include flowers, using vases, candles, stones, signs, etc. Even bridal bouquets can be made out of other items, including feathers and vintage brooches. You can also make your own "flowers" out of pretty paper or even coffee filters, if you'd like.

OFFICIANT

Frugal Wedding

Officiant

National Average Cost: $260+

This is one part of your wedding that you can't do yourself! Depending on where you live and your religious preferences, it can be hard to find someone to officiate your wedding. The best way to start is with a simple online search for officiants in your area. This will pull up several wedding vendor sites where you can check out their credentials and reviews and see if they're willing to travel to your venue. This is also a great source if you're looking for alternative officiants that will provide non-religious ceremonies.

No matter where you find an officiant, spend some time talking to them and making sure they can provide the service you're looking for. Ministers or other religious officials may be a little be more conservative or have certain rules they must follow that don't fit in with your dream wedding, so ask for specific details. If you can, get a copy of the ceremony in writing. This ensures that everyone is on the same page, and it gives you and your fiancee a chance to go over it in detail.

Ask A Friend
Your Frugal Wedding Budget: $0

The American Fellowship Church, Universal Life Church, along with other online ministries, will ordain just about anyone to officiate a wedding. HOWEVER, call the registrar in the township where your wedding will be held before your friend becomes ordained, because municipalities can vary as to whom they legally recognize as a wedding officiant.

KEEP YOUR CASH TIPS

Courthouse or Town/City Hall - Give your local courthouse or city hall a call. They may be able to direct you to a low cost justice of the peace, notary public, officiant, or retired judge who can perform the ceremony.

Explore Within Your Faith - If you and/or your fiancee are religious, you can probably find someone within your church who is willing to help you out, either for free or a small fee.

THE PHOTOGRAPHER

Frugal Wedding

Photographer

National Average Cost: $2,400+

---

*I*f you've priced out wedding photographers, you already know that this aspect of your wedding can blow your modest budget in an instant. But this is one of the few wedding aspects that definitely can't be done by you, and really can't be done by a family member or friend either because you want them in the pictures too! So how do you have a $1500 wedding without spending it all on a photographer?

Find a Beginner
Your Frugal Wedding Budget: $200

Consider finding a photographer on CraigsList or at a local college who is just starting out. Often he or she will be happy to do your wedding for a couple hundred dollars just to build their portfolio. Ideally, they will already have at least a few samples of their work for you to look at, which will make you feel more comfortable with hiring them.

KEEP YOUR CASH TIPS

Friends of Friends - Photography is a very popular hobby these days. Ask everyone you know to ask everyone they know to try to find someone who is an amateur photographer who would be willing to shoot your wedding for a couple hundred dollars. Be sure to ask:

- to see samples of their portrait work, either on social media or via email
- what kind of camera they use, to make sure it's a high-end digital
- when and how they will send you your pictures

Keep It Short - Reduce the amount of billable hours for your photographer by scheduling important events like toasts, cutting the cake, and tossing the bouquet as early in the reception as possible. That way the photographer can get all of the shots you need and leave, rather than staying for the entire evening.

Fight for Your Right... to Print? Many wedding photographers will charge you for their services, and then make you pay again for the right to get prints. Of your photos. Of YOUR wedding.

The thing is, technically they have the right to do that, because photography is covered by intellectual property laws: Whoever takes the picture owns all of the rights to that picture.

What that means, is that when hiring a wedding photographer - especially if they're an amateur or beginner - you have to make it clear that you want a USB or DVD with all of the digital images taken on your Big Day, along with an understanding (perhaps even in writing) that you have the right to print any and all of those pictures as many times as your big wonderful heart desires. Remember that the photographer will still retain intellectual ownership of those pictures, however, and - especially if they are a beginner - they will likely use pictures from your wedding on their website.

Edit, Print, and Scrapbook Yourself - Even beginner photographers will most likely charge you extra for editing your photos. Prints and albums will also cost you extra if ordered through your photographer - far more than getting them printed at WalMart, CVS, or online printing websites like SnapFish and Picaboo. Let whoever is taking your pictures know that you will handle all of this yourself, and all you want from them are HIGH-RESOLUTION digital files.

A Group Effort - In today's current age of smartphones, you can also provide a few close friends or family with a specific list of simple pictures you'd like taken (cake, guests seated, sweetheart table, centerpieces, etc.). Be careful though - this should be a COMPLEMENT to your hired photographer, NOT a replacement. This day is just too important to miss capturing it on film. A friend of mine opted for the "disposable cameras on the tables" route, and she ended up with about a hundred pictures of her and her new husband walking into their reception and not much else.

Know What You Want - Whoever does your photography, do some research and make note of shots and poses that you like, and share them with your photographer. Even the experts like a little insight into exactly what you want. The only way to get that perfect shot is to let everyone know about it beforehand.

Make a Schedule - Keep in mind that there are probably a lot of pictures that you would like to have taken, and it might be difficult to squeeze it all in during your wedding. You'll miss out on time mingling with your guests and enjoying the party. Consider having the wedding portraits taken before the ceremony when the other guests haven't arrived yet. Note that this doesn't work if you are a traditional couple and you don't want to see each other before the ceremony.

Another key problem when it comes to wedding portraits is making sure everyone is there when you need them. Let both sides of the family know when they'll be needed for pictures. You don't have time to be chasing down soon-to-be in-laws!

THE MUSIC

Frugal Wedding

Music

National Average Cost: $5,000+

---

*E*ver since you were little, you've dreamed of your first dance as a married couple - but you probably never worried about who would be in charge of playing the music. Music provides a soundtrack for your wedding, with songs that are important to you and say something about your relationship. Paying for a wedding band or a DJ can take a hefty chunk out of any budget, but we live in a time where you have other options.

Digital DJ
Your Frugal Wedding Budget: $0

Many brides-to-be are skipping the formality of an actual DJ and simply downloading their favorite music onto an iPod or other digital device. Then you just have to bring in a speaker or two and hit play! If you do decide to have an iPod wedding, make sure you have someone assigned to manage it. Just because you have all the perfect songs loaded onto it doesn't mean they'll play exactly when you need them to. Ask a friend or family member who's familiar with the device to be in charge of the soundtrack for your wedding. Also, make sure the songs are loaded onto a playlist in the correct order so there's less chance of a mess-up.

KEEP YOUR CASH TIPS

DJ on the Cheap - Check Craigslist or other local listings for college students who might be willing to DJ for a few bucks and a free meal. You can also try calling university campus centers and asking if they've hired any student DJs recently.

Live Music - Wedding bands can be a lot of fun but are very expensive. Luckily, there are a lot of options that are easier on your budget:

- *Less is More* - Instead of going straight for a group of musicians, consider one or two instruments. Why hire a full string quartet for your ceremony when you can get just as much romance and fullness of sound with a solo cello? You may need to pay a little extra because the musician has to do all of the work, but it will still be less than an ensemble. Just pick your instrument wisely: A harp may look and sound ethereal and romantic, but it's actually generally more expensive because of the hassle of transportation.
- *Local Talent* - Decide what kind of music you want (jazz, rock, traditional folk music, classical, etc.) and then call around to local bars, restaurants, and clubs to find out if there are any groups performing in your genre of choice. If you like what you hear, approach them about performing at your wedding. Be sure to ask where they're based - musicians will often

charge more if they have to travel more than an hour to get to your venue.

- *Local Schools* - Call up music schools in your area and ask if there are any faculty who are interested, or any students who have the professionalism and performance capability. Be sure to meet with any students before giving them the gig, and don't be afraid to ask them to play for you as an audition.

REHEARSAL DINNER & POST-WEDDING BRUNCH

Rehearsal Dinner & Post-Wedding Brunch

National Average Cost: $1,100+

---

*A*s much as we'd like to skip the expense, rehearsal the day before is necessary. If you want your day to run smoothly and stress-free, then you definitely need to get everyone in the wedding party together to run through the logistics. This is particularly important if friends and family will be helping with things like table and chair setup, music duties, and officiating. At the same time, the post-wedding brunch is a perfect way to thank out-of-town guests for traveling, and say goodbye. Unfortunately, both of these activities can cost a lot, and these costs need to be included in your wedding budget.

The good news is that lots of the same cost-saving strategies that apply to your wedding can also help you save on your rehearsal dinner and brunch.

BYOBBQ
Your Frugal Wedding Budget: $100

A backyard Bring Your Own Barbecue works for either the rehearsal or as a replacement for the brunch. You buy the burgers, and ask everyone else to bring everything else. It's a great way for everyone to relax just before (or after) the Big Day, and it is loads cheaper than a traditional formal meal.

KEEP YOUR CASH TIPS

Bare Essentials Guest List - The rehearsal dinner has ballooned in recent years into an event including nearly as many people as the wedding day itself. For those Happy Couples keeping their costs low, the only people you should invite to your rehearsal dinner are those in the wedding party.

Depending on the number of out-of-town guests you have, you might be able to include them too; if there are too many to invite, let them know that you're keeping the rehearsal dinner to wedding party and immediate families only, and you'll be having a post-wedding brunch that they're invited to. You can even limit the brunch to out-of-towners only, or out-of-towners and immediate family only, leaving out bridesmaids and groomsmen, since you probably see them all the time anyway.

Skip the Full Meal - Schedule your rehearsal earlier in the day. Get a bunch of friends together the day before and make finger sandwiches and brownies. Afternoon tea is a perfect theme for this type of gathering.

Leftovers - If you took home a refrigerator's worth of leftovers from your wedding, invite everyone over to help you clear it all out, rather than spending money on a post-wedding brunch.

Think Outside the Dinner Box - Instead of feeding everyone, pay for a fun night or afternoon at the bowling alley or mini golf range. Or go the free route: pack up the bocce ball or cornhole set and have everyone join you for a BYOP (picnic) at a nearby park. Activities like this are a relaxing and unique way for the in-laws and wedding party to get to know each other better. If it's your rehearsal, you might have trouble getting everyone to focus on the task at hand, so you might want to get the logistics out of the way *before* blowing them all away with your kickball skills.

FINAL THOUGHTS

Frugal Wedding

GREENBACK WEDDING

*I*t's not possible to talk about your wedding budget without talking about having a "greenback" wedding; meaning, asking for cash from your guests instead of traditional gifts. Some tactful ways of asking for money include:

- *Word of Mouth* - Tell friends and family that if anyone asks them, you'd like cash instead of gifts.
- *Online Cash Registries* - There are lots of websites that offer cash registries, like Honeyfund or MyRegistry, and these are a great way to direct your guests to specific goals you'd appreciate some help funding (like your honeymoon!).
- *Keep it Optional* - Some guests will still want to get you a regular gift, so create a traditional online gift registry as well. Be thoughtful with your gift registry; this is a great way to suggest items that you would have spent money on anyway, freeing up more of your cash for you and your sweetie's new life together.

LET'S RECAP

Here's the same chart from Chapter One, outlining the excessive national average costs of a wedding:

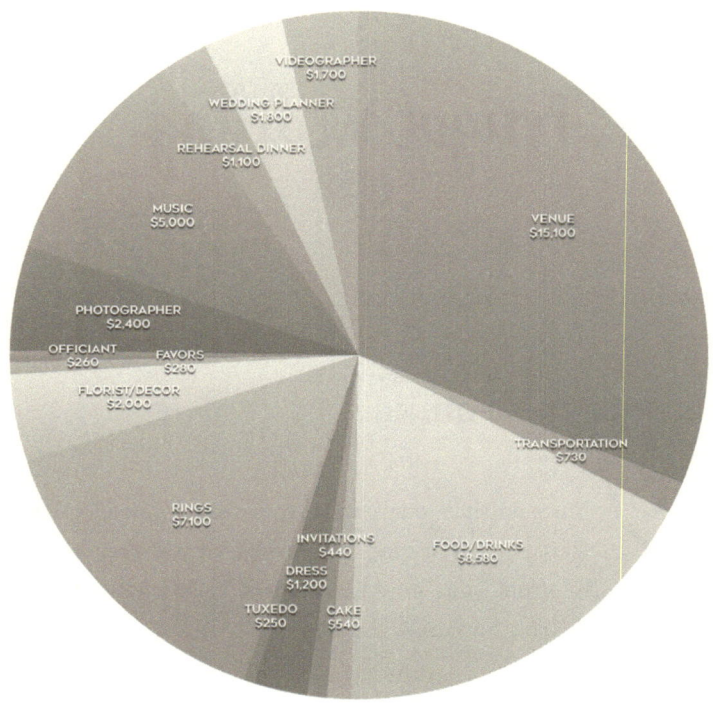

National Average Wedding Costs in the USA

Now, here's a chart outlining the costs of *Your Frugal Wedding* Budget:

venue - $300

tables/chairs - $50

transportation - $0

food/drinks - $300

cake - $130

invitations - $75

dress - 150

tux - $0

rings - $50

shoes/accessories - $0

decor - $50

favors - $50

guest book - $20

card box - $5

flowers - $20

officiant - $0

photographer - $200

music - $0

rehearsal dinner/post-wedding brunch - $100

=$1500

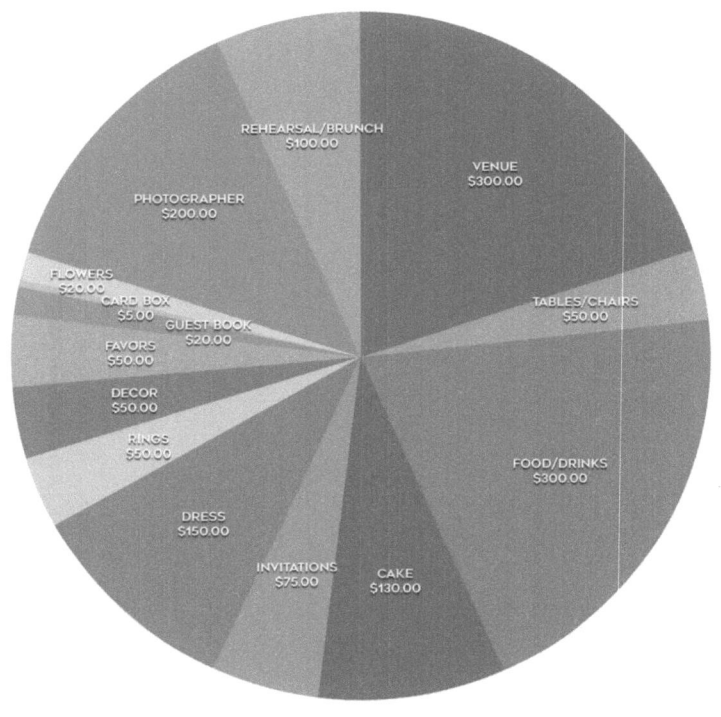

Your Frugal Wedding Costs

Much better!

Again, everything on here is fluid depending on your priorities, opportunities, and connections. Know someone who can shoot your wedding for free? Score! Add that $200 to your dress budget. Did your father-in-law offer to pay for the venue? Cool! Maybe you can hire that solo acoustic guitarist for the ceremony! The goal of this book is to show you that it truly is possible to have a fun, romantic wedding and not pay for it later. Literally.

GOOD LUCK!

Does it seem like there's an awful lot to think about and way too many decisions to make? Relax. That's how every couple feels regardless of their budget. Just make sure you set aside a little bit of time each week to discuss arrangements or do some shopping, and you'll have it all put together in no time.

This book has shown you many ways to save money for your wedding. There is no part of a wedding that you can't get for a better price, or perhaps even for free. Don't settle on anything that costs more than you're willing to pay. After all, it's your money and your day!

The bottom line here is that you should not feel ashamed or stressed because you want your wedding to come in at a reasonable amount. Budget weddings are far more common than you may realize, and they are a product of careful planning and great amounts of personal effort. It may take a little more time, but it's definitely worth it.

Having an economical wedding does not mean that you have to make sacrifices on aesthetics, fun, or style. If anything, it means that you have put a little bit more time and effort into each aspect of your wedding, choosing elements that reflect your personalities.

So invite your friends and family to help you, seek out the best available prices for everything, and start planning. Remember, every penny you save can be put towards your fun honeymoon getaway!

And congratulations again! Thank you, and good luck!

Frugal Wedding

Amazon Warehouse Deals

FatWallet

My Wedding Favors

Online Wedding Registry

Raise

❧

and our own site:

YOUR FRUGAL WEDDING:
www.yourfrugalwedding.com

ABOUT THE AUTHOR

Frugal Wedding

Rachel Hathaway is the pen name for a professional writer whom you may or may not know (Mysterious, huh?). Her work spans many areas of creative fiction -- including the very wide romance genre -- as well as her published non-fiction self-help guides, personal growth and development ebooks, and a large number of articles and posts across the web on a variety of sites and blogs about smart modern shopping, style, music, the arts, and a range of eco-friendly topics. She lives in New England with her devoted in their dream home, and they make sure to enjoy the wonderful aspects of life on a daily basis.

Finally, if you enjoyed this book, please take the time to share your thoughts and post a review where you bought it, because most people don't. If you do, it'd be greatly appreciated!

For more information and to join our mailing list:

www.yourfrugalwedding.com

ALSO BY RACHEL HATHAWAY

Updated Paleo Diet Food List (Plus Paleo Diet Shopping Lists) *[Also in paperback, audiobook, and in Spanish and Danish ebook translations]*

Beginner's Guide to Writing and Self-Publishing Romance eBooks (New Romance Writer Series) *[Also in paperback]*

Minimalism for Moms: Simplify, Declutter, and Organize Your Way to a Stress Free and Meaningful Life (Serenity at Home)

The Unofficial History of Flirting: Plus Five Ways to Reinvent Valentine's Day and Flirt Like a Bird! (Sassy Girl Series) *[Also in paperback]*

⁂

SPANISH TRANSLATIONS (with Elisa Prada, translator):

Lista de alimentos para la dieta Paleo: Actualizado / Spanish Language Edition (Updated Paleo Diet Food List Book) (Serie de Nutrición) (Spanish Edition) *[Also in paperback]*

Minimalismo para Mamás: Simplifica, arregla, y organiza tu camino hacia una vida plena libre de estrés (Minimalism for Moms / Spanish edition) (Serie Serenidad en el Hogar)

Frugal Wedding

NOTES & IDEAS:

AFTERWORD

THANK YOU AGAIN for downloading this 3-book set!

I hope this book was able to help you to plan your wedding under budget, understand the Paleo diet, and recover your serenity at home — whether you are a mom now or will be sometime soon or on the future.

The next step is to take action with all the information contained here!

Finally, if you enjoyed this book, please take the time to share your thoughts and post a review where you purchased the book. It would be greatly appreciated!

Thank you and good luck!

ALSO BY RACHEL HATHAWAY

Updated Paleo Diet Food List (Plus Paleo Diet Shopping Lists)

Beginner's Guide to Writing and Self-Publishing Romance eBooks (New Romance Writer Series) *[Also in paperback]*

Minimalism for Moms: Simplify, Declutter, and Organize Your Way to a Stress Free and Meaningful Life (Serenity at Home)

The Unofficial History of Flirting: Plus Five Ways to Reinvent Valentine's Day and Flirt Like a Bird! (Sassy Girl Series) *[Also in paperback]*

❧

SPANISH TRANSLATIONS (Elisa Prada, translator):

Lista de alimentos para la dieta Paleo: Actualizado / Spanish Language Edition (Updated Paleo Diet Food List Book) (Serie de Nutrición) (Spanish Edition) *[Also in paperback]*

Minimalismo para Mamás: Simplifica, arregla, y organiza tu camino hacia una vida plena libre de estrés (Minimalism for Moms / Spanish edition) (Serie Serenidad en el Hogar)

www.ingramcontent.com/pod-product-compliance
Lightning Source LLC
Chambersburg PA
CBHW050444290526
45786CB00006B/2153